THE OFFSHORE PRIVACY MANUAL

by

Adam Starchild

International Law and Taxation Publishers

The Offshore Privacy Manual

by
Adam Starchild

ISBN 1-893713-12-1

Copyright © 2000 by Adam Starchild

International Law & Taxation Publishers
London
http://www.internationallawandtaxationpublishers.com

Contents

Chapter One

A Broad Overview: Wealth & Privacy Issues

For as long as history records the progress of mankind, people have been searching for ways to increase their wealth and improve their standard of living. This is largely what separates man from his predecessors — the ability to control one's own destiny. Unfortunately, both the acquisition and preservation of wealth are constantly under scrutiny by governments, competitors, and predators wanting to share the spoils.

For every individual intent on accumulating wealth, there are hundreds of others trying to impede his progress. If your personal goal has been to amass a sizeable portfolio to assure yourself and your family a bright future, you should consider that you probably have numerous enemies trying this very minute to defeat your efforts. Some have been elected to Congress. Others have been appointed to the judiciary. Many undoubtedly work at 1600 Pennsylvania Avenue in Washington.

But it doesn't stop there. Millions of people less fortunate than you are also represented by lobbyists and attorneys in *their* quest to get their hands on your assets. We used to call them *pirates* but today they act within the bounds of law. They demand that you share your portfolio through income equalization programs. Those who are really bold will take you to court in an effort to have your assets seized so that the money can be spread around.

In an effort to live better, modern society has fostered all sorts of innovative tools and technologies. Most historians and sociologists agree that we now live in an *information age* where news and knowledge have become more important keys to wealth building than productivity or other traditional economic factors of production like land, labor, and capital. As a result, we need to guard information against pilferage in the same way we guard our other assets. Many of us have become cavalier, if not downright reckless, in the way we allow our most personal financial records to be publicly exposed.

The historic search for wealth, and now the contemporary search for information, have created many problems as well as opportunities. Those who have significant assets naturally want to protect them against natural erosion or intentional theft. On the other hand, individuals with limited assets look to government as *the great equalizer*, hoping that it will reallocate capital from the *haves* to the *have-nots* through various social programs.

The Theory Of Economic Relativity

Wealth and information are both *relative* commodities. It isn't what you have that it important; it is what you have relative to others that counts. There are no absolute yardsticks to measure personal or corporate wealth. We become rich only when our financial wealth significantly exceeds the wealth of others in our society. If everyone was a millionaire, being a millionaire would not even insure our ability to meet the basic necessities of life.

The same is true of information and knowledge. A person isn't deemed *smart* because he has accumulated some absolute quantity of factual information. He is considered smart only when his knowledge base materially surpasses that of his contemporaries. We measure intelligence in a similar way using scoring techniques in which an intelligence quotient of 100 is assigned to a person with *average* intelligence. When individuals compete for professional licensure by examination in a wide array of fields, they are *normatively* scored. The passing grade is often based on the average of all test takers.

As an example, registered nurse applicants who score less than one standard deviation below the norm on national examinations receive a failing grade; the rest go on to treat us in health care facilities. Hopefully, if you are ever hospitalized, you will be cared for by a nurse who took her examination among a relatively smart group of applicants. If you were a graduating nursing student, the lesson might be *not* to study or cram for the examination with your colleagues. After all, the higher their grades, the lower yours becomes using relative or normative scoring. The lesson for the rest of us who are not going into nursing is that being just a little smarter than our contemporaries is the key to long-term financial success. A corollary might be in order, too. If you find an unusually effective strategy for achieving your personal or professional goals, keep it to yourself.

The investor who makes money in the stock market does so because his information is a little better or a little more timely than someone else's. The same holds true for the successful small business owner or the rare gambler who consistently beats the odds at the horse track. Those who are able to maintain a privacy edge over their friends and colleagues stand a better chance of reaching their lifelong objectives. Economies which encourage that extra bit of capital investment or productivity run rings around those that remain complacent. Life is not unlike parimutuel wagering. One man's loss is another man's gain.

An acquaintance who happens to be a physician tells the story of a successful businessman who was so obsessed with wealth accumulation and immortality that he directed his family to freeze his body when he learned that he had contracted a deadly disease for which there was no current cure. Years later the man found himself in a hospital room, gradually thawing out from a thirty-year respite in a cryogenic state. A doctor delivered the good news that a cure had been found for the viral infection that had nearly killed the patient three decades earlier.

As he left the hospital, the businessman called his broker to check on the state of his investments. He received a second round of good news. His portfolio which had been valued at two million dollars when he first became ill was now worth well over a hundred million. He hailed a cab to take him home so he could pick up the pieces and get on with his life.

When the cab pulled up to his home just twenty minutes later, he sighed and smiled, dreaming of all the things he could do with a hundred million dollars. The taxi driver quickly looked at the meter and announced the cab fare.

"Sir, that will be $10,285," he said nonchalantly.

A million dollars, a hundred million dollars, even a billion dollars may not be all that impressive unless it has value in the broader context of economic relativity. We need to consider the effects of inflation, purchasing power, and taxes among many other things in determining real wealth. While inflation may play havoc with creditors, it is a joy for debtors who can pay their bills with devalued future dollars. Wealth building and wealth maintenance are not the simple processes they used to be. Today they require the application of new sophisticated global strategies. It is no longer enough to amass a small fortune. Keeping it out of the hands of predators requires careful planning.

The Information Age

Just as there is a perpetual class struggle for financial wealth, there is also an ongoing fight over information. Governments have often been called in to regulate the process by which information is disseminated. In the United States, for example, the Securities and Exchange Commission oversees filing requirements of publicly-traded corporations. In the interests of fairness, corporations are required to disclose many facts about their operations, their current and historic performance, even the backgrounds of their directors and officers. Practices such as insider trading are in some countries forbidden by law and punishable by severe criminal and civil penalties. The idea is to provide a supposedly even playing field for both the small investor and the big corporate giant. The question is *even for whom?*

In practice, laws provide very little protection for those who need protection the most. The Fair Credit Reporting Act, for example, provides a mechanism for individuals to review and correct credit reports which contain erroneous information — misinformation which can destroy an individual's ability to secure loans or other forms of credit. On the other hand, credit reporting agencies have become relatively immune from lawsuits arising out of bad information in their files. They have taken the position that they are mere *repositories* of information which they do not guarantee to be correct — and the courts have largely agreed with them. Once you furnish information to others whether willingly, reluctantly, or unknowingly, you are no longer in possession or control of that information. Those who have it can largely use it as they see fit.

Federal Government Intrusion

Other federal laws with equally misleading names included the Bank Secrecy Act of 1970 which did anything but guarantee bank secrecy. What it did was to open all American bank records to the government, requiring financial institutions among other things to microfilm all checks and deposit slips in excess of $100. Still worse, Section 5313 of the Bank Secrecy Act imposed on banks the duty to file Currency Transaction Reports (IRS Form 4789) for each deposit, withdrawal, or currency exchange exceeding $10,000. Casinos were ordered to file Currency Transaction Reports by Casinos (IRS Form 8362) for similar-sized transactions. Winners, of course, were required to annually report their gambling earnings as income; losers could only claim their losses to the extent of winnings in any given year, losses against other income disallowed. Businesses were directed to IRS Form 8300 under the provisions of Section 60501 of the IRS Code to report their monetary transactions.

Additional provisions forced Americans to declare the transport of cash, negotiable securities, and other monetary instruments across U.S. borders. Section 5316 of the Banking Secrecy Act created the Currency or

Monetary Instrument Report (U.S. Customs Service Form 4790). The original $5000 threshold was later raised to $10,000 when the government realized it was burying itself in paperwork.

Perhaps most unpalatable was the new reporting requirement for Americans to disclose the existence of banking and related financial accounts outside the United States. When the total of funds held offshore exceeds $10,000, detailed descriptions of the accounts and locations must be furnished on U.S. Department of Treasury Form TDR 90-22-1, the Foreign Bank Account Report.

The law didn't stop there, however. Federal lawmakers had so broadly defined the concept of a *financial institution* as to embrace virtually any business through which money passed as well as other businesses and professions only tangentially related to money. Banks, savings and loan associations, brokers, title companies, currency exchanges, credit card issuers, traveler's check and money order sellers, and even the U.S. Post Office in effect became agents of the U.S. government. Even accountants, attorneys, and other fiduciary advisors found themselves in the clutches of Uncle Sam. The very people who were supposed to represent and advise you confidentially are now at risk of losing their licenses to practice, not to mention federal criminal prosecution.

To make certain that it left no stone unturned, the government further defined a financial institution to include any entity whose reporting would be useful in the administration of criminal, tax, or regulatory matters. In effect, that left nobody untouched. Washington had declared war on personal financial privacy.

Naturally, the government's position was challenged in the courts. Uncle Sam won each round. In California Bankers Association v Schultz, a plaintiff alleged that his bank had violated his Fifth Amendment rights against self-incrimination as well as his Fourth Amendment rights against unreasonable search and seizure. The case worked it way up to the U.S. Supreme

Court but the government prevailed. Bank records, the courts ruled, were the property of the bank and not the individual customer.

Justice William O. Douglas wrote a strongly-worded dissenting opinion in which he criticized the federal government for trampling on individual civil liberties, using a *sledge-hammer approach* when a *delicate scalpel* would do in the quest to catch criminals. Although the issue of privacy continued to surface in the years since 1970, frequently during U.S. Senate confirmation hearings for proposed Supreme Court justices, little was ever actually accomplished in Congress to restore or at least prevent the further erosion of individual privacy rights. On the contrary, laws like the Privacy Act of 1974 and the Right to Financial Privacy Act of 1978 were so filled with exclusions as to render them worthless.

Fortunately, the rest of the world's governments did not immediately follow suit, though many found themselves under extreme pressure if not duress by the American government. The Kerry Amendment to the Anti-Drug Abuse Act of 1988 was such an example of America's attempts at international extortion. It ordered that foreign governments, as if they were not sovereign nations in their own right, report cash deposits of $10,000 or more by American nationals in their banks. The President of the United States was directed to impose sanctions against nations failing to cooperate. This was not the first time Washington chose to bully the rest of the world and it certainly would not be the last.

Although many nations entered into compacts with Washington, some of which allowed their banks to disclose information when American authorities could demonstrate criminal activity, the right to privacy was still available to Americans doing business in many offshore jurisdictions. Today, certain types of offshore accounts still fall outside the grips of America's prying government. As an overall rule of thumb, you are likely to enjoy some far more serious measures of bank secrecy almost anywhere in the world compared to the United States.

The complex web of American laws and regulations is almost impossible to fathom. In almost all cases, these laws and regulations were purportedly enacted to protect society but often at the serious expense of individual freedom. Each one of us has a somewhat different idea what it means to keep the scales of justice in balance. It is impossible to gain consensus on how much government is appropriate and how much government is oppressive. To some extent, any individual or corporate judgment of this issue depends on time and place. Even America's most conservative individuals and corporations have changed position one hundred eighty degrees when it was advantageous for them to do so.

Most Fortune 500 executives, for example, have long argued that government ought to keep its nose out of the business sector. When, on the other hand, Chrysler Corporation appeared ready to hit the financial skids a few years ago, its chairman begged Congress for loan guarantees to keep it afloat. Lee Iacocca warned Washington that without loan guarantees, tens of thousands of workers might be forced out of work, severely impacting the nation's economy.

We had rarely heard corporate chairman complaining about rank-and-file workers losing their jobs before this and we haven't heard the message again since Congress acquiesced to the loan guarantees. In fact, every corporate layoff in recent memory has been accompanied by a significant rise in stock price. What's good for Wall Street is not necessarily good for Main Street. The message was clear, however. Congressional meddling is generally objectionable but it is quite all right when it provides immediate benefits to the affected party.

These kind of changing adversarial relationships underscore the problems inherent in accumulating and preserving wealth. What is good for your pocketbook may not necessarily be good for other people's pocketbooks. Moreover, strategies that were acceptable a few years ago may be totally inappropriate today. The love of country should not prevent you from examining attractive offshore alternatives that help you to preserve all that you have accumulated.

Chapter One

A Culture Develops

It's bad enough that we have allowed our own governments to deprive us of the rights of secrecy and anonymity in our financial dealings. We have unfortunately made the situation even worse by developing a national culture in which we not only tolerate, but condone, behaviors which let others steal from us.

An appellate court recently ruled that a defendant has no right to privacy in the trash he discards in front of his house or in the large metal container behind his business. The case arose when authorities, intent on getting a criminal conviction, arranged to have the man's household garbage sifted through for evidence. People always considered their homes off limits to unlawful searches and seizures, but who thought much about the trash left at the front curb? Now that we know that curbside trash is no longer the property of its original owner, we should be more far more careful in what we discard and how we obliterate or shred it. Unfortunately, many individuals and businesses are still blasé in this area.

In Florida, a television station reporter recently stumbled on a major find. One of the region's largest banks had contracted with a local firm for the disposal of canceled checks. Few checking account holders received their canceled checks any longer with their monthly statements. Instead, the checks are processed, microfiched, and then discarded. The paper is sold to recyclers in the name of profit and environmental protection. Unfortunately, the particular hauler in this case was making no effort to shred or otherwise render these checks unreadable. Hundreds were found laying in trash containers, jeopardizing the confidentiality of information they contained. The bank, when questioned by the reporter, declined to comment on its practices.

A few years ago, a business acquaintance ordered a couple of boxes of floppy disks from a major mail-order computer supply company. They arrived a few days later by UPS. He noticed that the cellophane wrapping on one of the packages had been broken open and initially assumed that it had merely come undone in a warehouse. To his utter amazement he found that one of the disks in the opened package actually contained thousands of bytes of information in tabular form — information from a Texas-based financial institution. When he complained to the mail-order retailer, he was told that the box of disks had evidently been returned by another customer, perhaps as the wrong size. They made good on the order by sending my colleague a couple of additional free boxes of diskettes.

So incensed by the situation, the recipient of this information-laden diskette reported the matter to both state and federal authorities. Neither appeared the least bit interested that confidential banking information had been compromised by the bank. To paraphrase their responses — *erase the data and get on with your work.*

Nowhere else in the world would the negligent and reckless release of bank records like this be tolerated by public authorities. Complacency as well as intentional intrusions into the privacy of individuals and businesses have become a way of life in the United States.

Big Brother's Computers

In an effort to manipulate or allocate wealth, many government agencies accumulate massive data bases. These are used to carry out duties including tax collection and compliance, law enforcement, health and safety administration, and a host of others. Recent events in Washington and elsewhere prove that government agencies cannot be trusted to use their information collecting authority in a lawful or ethical manner. Internal Revenue Service files have been repeatedly misused for political purposes, the IRS specifically targeting individuals and businesses they do not like. Even the supposedly sacred files of the Federal Bureau of Investigation have been compromised as demonstrated in the infamous 1986 White House scandal.

What is even more frightening is the fact that the various data bases are linked together in an elaborate framework which assures that Big Brother knows your every move. The Treasury Enforcement Communications System (TECS II) regularly receives data from lower-level computers at the Internal Revenue Service and U.S. Customs centers. It then processes the information using an artificial intelligence system, a sophisticated program designed to uncover patterns of suspicious financial transactions. An individual or business who makes successive deposits over several days or weeks, each of which falls well below the $10,000 reporting threshold, may thus be identified as trying to beat the system through an illegal activity known as *structuring*. A 1991 amendment to the Bank Secrecy Act made it illegal to break down payments in excess of $10,000 in order to avoid reporting requirements of law.

Practices affecting the dissemination of financial information not only reflect government's greed but sometimes its plain ignorance of what is morally right or prudent. The Social Security Administration, in a well-intentioned but utterly stupid attempt to make individual records more accessible to their respective taxpayers, recently established an interactive Internet web site. With minimal information such as a social security number and a mother's maiden name, virtually anyone could tap into anyone else's social security records. Nobody knows how many unwarranted intrusions occurred before Washington pulled the plug on the web site so that a comprehensive study could be undertaken. It seems bad enough that government has often abused its powers by misusing information it has gathered on individuals; now the information is being recklessly disseminated to others with questionable motives.

Virtually all financial transactions made in the United States are tracked or at least trackable by the government. A social security number must be furnished to open a bank account, obtain a mortgage or loan, or trade a financial security. In many states, social security numbers are also assigned to drivers licenses (and a new federal law will make social security numbers on drivers' licenses mandatory within the next few years). Colleges and universities typically track student grades using these same nine-digit identifiers. Merchants and credit card companies furnish credit reporting agencies with millions of bits of information or misinformation daily, all neatly filed away by social security number. Applications for health and life insurance policies are routinely scanned by underwriters who examine medical records with a fine tooth comb, again accessing these histories by social security number.

Share Your Social Security Number And Lose Everything

Try to fill a prescription in San Diego and you will have to furnish a social security number to the pharmacy. It will be entered into a computer and stored somewhere in cyberspace. Drive across the border to Tijuana and you will not only get your medicine without a social security number; you will get it without a prescription, without disclosing your name, and for half the price. The avoidance of a prescription trail may be very important to someone with a so-called pre-existing condition which prevents him from obtaining health insurance.

The death of privacy has admittedly created many cottage industries. A host of people-finding services has spring up in recent years. For a small fee, usually under fifty dollars, such businesses can locate almost anyone from public records as well as the files of credit reporting agencies. Furnish a social security number and you are virtually guaranteed a comprehensive report. These firms provide information on current and former addresses, employment histories, and much more. Similar services provide background checks for employers seeking to hire personnel. Arrest records are typically public. Landlords desiring information on prospective tenants can also turn to such information bureaus to assess potential risk.

It's no wonder that thousands of Americans have literally had their identities *lifted* by thieves who steal their social security numbers and then obtain credit cards in their victims' names. The victims often suffer for years, unable to clear their adverse credit histories created by their clones. Is this what is meant by *being beside yourself?*

Invasion of privacy by both government and private-sector interests is rampant. Nothing in the Constitution of the United States explicitly guarantees individuals the right to privacy, making it all the more necessary to protect your own interests. Although most people seem to agree in principle that privacy is an implicit natural right, judicial interpretations have wavered over the years and nobody knows what the future will bring. The overall trend is clearly one marked by increased government intrusion on individuals.

Electronic Eavesdropping

Laws affecting privacy are a patchwork of piecemeal legislation. In theory it is unlawful in the United States to eavesdrop on cellular phone conversations or to sell new equipment designed to pick up these transmissions. It is well known on the street, however, that old receivers can be easily converted to pick up these frequencies as House Speaker Newt Gingrich painfully discovered when his comments about his agreement with the House Ethics Committee were recorded by a Florida couple and leaked to Congressional adversaries and then the *New York Times*. Maybe the incident will stimulate the sale of more sophisticated cellular phones which digitally scramble the signals.

With few exceptions, almost anything sent over the Internet also lacks security, forcing many businesses to begin encrypting sensitive email communications. In response to this, several foreign governments have forbidden the use of encryption software for email or telephone conversations. It is unlawful for Americans to export some of the strongest encryption software without a license, the same kind of license required for the export of arms and munitions.

Washington lawmakers are pushing for legislation which would require all encryption software manufacturers to hand over to the government the *electronic keys* which actually secure these programs, effectively allowing the government to eavesdrop on encrypted email and telephone conversations. This would be analogous to a law requiring the creation of one master key which could open every home, business, and safe deposit box in America — a key given to the FBI or some other agency.

Maintaining privacy is fundamental to maintaining strong personal financial security. We know that there are many danger signals on the horizon beyond the invasions of privacy which have already occurred. Politicians have been talking about the issuance of national identity cards, perhaps containing fingerprints or other uniquely identifiable data. The American military has already begun a process of cataloging DNA samples from all personnel, presumably to help identify casualty remains. In the wrong hands, these kinds of data can also be used by insurers to deny coverage to people predisposed to illness at some later date far in the future. If for example it is determined that a currently healthy woman has a gene which predisposes her to diabetes at some later date, an insurer may arbitrarily choose to deny health insurance coverage to reduce its risk of having to pay benefits.

One proposal that has abounded for years is the establishment of a national dental registry, presumably to help identify unknown corpses found in accidents and crime scenes. Dental records are currently used to positively identify victims whose teeth are compared to recorded X-rays and other observational records kept by dentists. At the present time, this requires locating the decedent's dental records. If a victim is truly unknown, this is a virtual impossibility The proposal would have given rise to a national library of dental records, yet another government data base established at an enormous cost to taxpayers.

For several years, the FBI has been requesting massive appropriations to exponentially increase its wiretap capabilities, purportedly in the fight against illegal drugs and organized crime. By some estimates, the expanded capacity would allow authorities in urban areas to eavesdrop on as many as *one in ten* phones at any given time. Phone companies would be required to install thousands of ports, an expense which would surely be passed along to consumers, to permit this kind of domestic spying. Which folks on your street will have their phones tapped?

If you work for a large corporation, you may well be the victim of a wiretap already. Many large companies routinely spy on their employees, listening in on phone conversations they make with customers and others. Sometimes this is done under the guise of *training*. More often it is done to challenge the loyalty of employees, to determine whether there are any dissenters among the ranks. Computer files and email are routinely scrutinized in these corporations by network administrators who have *carte blanche* to spy on their colleagues. Of course this policy not only allows executives to intrude on their workers, it gives them the freedom to spy on innocent third parties including customers and suppliers who may be doing business with their companies.

Several members of Congress have proposed legislative initiatives which would allow the introduction of evidence gathered in warrantless searches when the evidence was otherwise collected by police in good faith. Besides annulling the U.S. Constitution's prohibition on illegal searches and seizures, one should ask how we would determine what has been done in good faith. So-called *no-knock searches,* repeatedly challenged but upheld by the courts, have already eroded constitutional guarantees we used to take for granted. The authority was first given to private bounty hunters in their search for bail-jumpers, and more recently broadened to include a wide array of drug raids. The race is on to determine whether a criminal can flush a toilet faster than a DEA agent can knock down a door.

Seizures And Forfeitures

Americans now live in an environment where property seizures are rampant, where they have to prove themselves innocent before the eyes of the law in order to reclaim their assets. In many local jurisdictions, police use these new powers to seize cash, cars, boats, planes, real estate, and virtually anything else in their site with no regard for due process. Some local sheriffs boast that millions of dollars have been added to their coffers through such wild and reckless confiscations.

Cash found in vehicles during routine traffic stops is often confiscated and then scrutinized for the presence of trace quantities of cocaine or other illegal drugs. Given today's sensitive analytical techniques, laboratories can detect trace compounds that exist at concentrations less than one part per billion. By some estimates, fifty percent of all paper currency in circulation in the United States would now yield evidence of exposure to illegal drugs. The presumption of innocence is gone. Victims of such police scams now have to prove that the confiscated money had been lawfully obtained to reclaim it.

Many raids are now conducted without *probable cause*, a doctrine that protected Americans for two hundred years. People and vehicles are singled out for examination on the basis of *profiles* — the color and make of your car, the interstate road you travel, your apparent ethnicity, perhaps even the hat you wear.

With annual seizures now approaching $2 billion, government agencies are laughing all the way to the bank. Making matters worse is an old legal doctrine that has been resurrected to confiscate money and property from innocent third parties. Under the doctrine, the seized property is in effect found to be guilty of a crime despite the innocence of its owner. If you are a landlord whose tenant quietly and without your consent chooses to smoke marijuana, your rental property can be seized by government agents. An airline which carries passengers, one of whom fails to declare to customs a large purchase made overseas, can have its plane confiscated.

Large corporations can of course afford to challenge these actions in court. Individuals are often not that lucky. The IRS with the help of the U.S. Justice Department has often made it a practice to go after relatively insignificant cases, knowing that the litigants lack the financial resources necessary to fight big government, especially after their assets have been seized. The RICO statutes which were developed to fight organized racketeering and crime have been so broadly applied as to create a police state. The American Civil Liberties Union is in the minds of many Americans an unsavory organization that represents criminals. In truth, the ACLU is one of the few entities in America that continues to fight for constitutionally-guaranteed liberties.

We live in a society of competing interests. Some people cherish traditional values and constitutional protections while others are willing to sacrifice these liberties in the interests of short-term expediency. The decision when the means justify the ends is one that each person has to make for himself. What is uncontroverted is the fact that we are now on a very slippery slope with the potential for government abuse of innocent people monumental. The quest for privacy takes on a new sense of expediency as we seek to protect our hard-earned assets.

Life is like a series of chess games in which there are many adversaries. There will be winners and there will be losers. It is important to develop both strategic and operational plans to accomplish personal objectives including wealth accumulation and the protection of money and property from courts, creditors, and tax collectors. The more you own, the more you stand to lose by not developing appropriate plans now.

If you are smart enough to profit from your work or your investments, Big Brother will look to you for its share; if on the other hand you sustain losses, you will pretty much be on your own. New rules regarding losses from so-called passive activities have all but destroyed legitimate domestic tax shelters. Small business owners and entrepreneurs not only have to contend with government intrusions but also with competitors in the private sector. Intelligence gathering is a big business these days. It is remarkably easy to obtain proprietary information on both individuals and businesses whose assets are kept stateside. To the extent that you can shield your most sensitive financial and operational information from competitors, you will be able to maintain a significant edge over your competitors.

Creditors And Thieves

Court awards in many recent high-profile cases also underscore the importance of keeping assets out of the reach of adversaries. Compensatory and punitive judgments for civil liabilities are astronomical. In most cases insurance will not cover punitive or exemplary damages. A misspoken word or a bad business decision can cost millions in civil judgments.

You don't have to be an O. J. Simpson to have your assets attacked in court. People of modest means are ripe targets for suits. Take the case of a middle class American family whose home had been repeatedly broken into and vandalized in their absence. In an effort to protect their property in preparation for their next vacation, they added barbed wire to the top of their existing chain-link fence around the sides and back of their lot.

A burglar, exiting their home with a television set he had just stolen, was seriously injured by the barbed wire. The television came crashing to the ground below, the picture tube imploding with a big bang. Bleeding and in pain, the culprit was quickly apprehended by local police and charged with breaking and entering as well as burglary.

Despite his own troubles, the thief successfully sued the homeowners in civil court for his injuries, disfigurement, and pain and suffering. The court found that barbed wire represented a foreseeable danger and that the homeowners in any case were in violation of local codes in having installed it. Because of inadequate insurance protection, the homeowners were forced to liquidate assets including their home to pay the judgment issued by the court. A person's home is no longer his castle, at least in the United States.

As for the crimes of breaking and entering and burglary of a television, a separate criminal court handed the thief a suspended sentence. After all, it was his first felony conviction. It is no wonder Americans loathe the judicial system with a passion. A recent survey found that three out of four Americans don't trust the judiciary's ability to mete out justice fairly.

Accusations of product liability, discrimination, defamation, and even wrongful death are quite commonplace. Jury awards seem to have become limitless. Indeed, many plaintiffs now subscribe to the *deep pockets theory* in choosing their defendants; they go after parties from whom they are most likely to collect big sums.

Keeping assets offshore may not only prevent seizures in the event that judgments are made by courts but may actually deter costly litigation in the first place. Nobody wants to spend thousands of dollars to sue a defendant from whom it is impossible to collect. Even the government is likely to turn the other cheek in trying to collect small sums of money when it is forced to jump through successive hurdles just to access foreign bank records. Bureaucrats whose promotions depend on their collections success will look to easier targets to fill their assigned coffers.

Lose Your Money Quickly Or Slowly

If you are fortunate enough to escape the *acute* loss of assets through a judgment by creditors or a forfeiture by government agents, you are still likely to suffer a *chronic* loss of assets as a result of government policies that over the long run rob you of your hard-earned money. Unsavory politicians continue to take credit for all sorts of tax relief schemes, but the fact remains that all they have done is shuffle the deck a few times. When politicians nominally reduce one tax to win reelection, they invariably cause other taxes to rise in to offset the lost revenues.

It is very chic today for American politicians to talk about reducing big government programs in Washington. What happens more often than not is that the programs are merely turned over to the individual states which in turn have to raise their own revenues to fund all these new burdens.

Does it really matter if food stamps are doled out by Washington or alternatively by Tallahassee, Sacramento, and Albany?

Some states like California, Michigan, Wisconsin, and New York already tax their residents into near poverty. For many people, state and local taxes are more repressive than federal income taxes. Real estate taxes have driven many families out of their homes. State income taxes as well as local sales taxes make it difficult for many middle class people to survive. Even in death, the vultures of government descend with unconscionable inheritance taxes that prevent Americans from passing their wealth on to their spouses and children. It's no wonder Americans have one of the lowest personal savings rates in the entire industrialized world. When investment begins to dwindle, the national economy is in serious trouble.

Other nations are somewhat more progressive in their thinking. Britons who do not normally reside in the United Kingdom do not pay income tax to their home government, allowing them to accumulate wealth more rapidly. This seems fair because they do not avail themselves of many domestic services while they are living abroad. Offshore investments continue to grow through compounding.

It's not only the British, of course, who encourage wealth building. Similar laws throughout Europe, Latin America, and Asia encourage individuals to invest offshore. The net result of the disparity between their laws and American laws will have far-reaching effects in the near-term future.

Historically, one thing is rather certain. Whenever governments becomes heavy-handed in collecting unnecessary taxes, the result is predictable. It doesn't really matter whether taxes are collected to build national monuments or simply for purposes of wealth distribution and welfare programs. Heavy taxation always reduces investment capital as it reduces the incentive to plow money back into the economy. Productivity slips, jobs are lost, and the overall standard of living declines. In the end, investors living in jurisdictions with little or no tax liability will control the world's wealth. Americans and those living under similarly repressive tax structures will be left out in the cold.

Any individual with significant assets should assess his own situation carefully. His decisions today will determine where he and his family will be tomorrow. It isn't enough to simply find that you are doing all right. Economists frequently talk about *opportunity costs*. Simply stated, you have to consider your current position relative to what you *could* be earning under different scenarios. If, for example, you owned a rental property but through oversight failed to rent it out, you should consider the rents you never collected to be an economic loss. If you are an executive earning $200,000 a year but could have earned $350,000 annually by jumping ship and going into your own business, you sustained an economic loss of $150,000.

Similarly, you should examine your current after-tax income stream from cash investments in banks, stocks, bonds, mutual funds, or other investment vehicles. On first blush, you may consider yourself lucky in today's economic environment to be earning 6.0% after tax on your current investments. But what if you could raise the after-tax yield to 10, 12, 15, or even 24 percent by investing offshore? If you could earn 15% but didn't avail yourself of this opportunity, the reality is that you have lost 9%, the difference between what you could have earned and what you actually earned. If a 24% return was attainable — and this is not out of the question with strong investment advice — you lost 18% by taking comfort in your present mediocre situation.

The effects of compounding are profound. Take a $100,000 lump sum investment over a twenty-year period. At 6.0% interest compounded annually, your money would grow to $320,000. Raise the yield to 10% and you will have accumulated $672,750 in twenty years. At 12%, your investment would reach a total value of $964,629 and at 24% you would boast a whopping $7,386,416. Naturally, the earlier you get started, the more you have to gain. Offshore investing provides opportunities for this kind of accelerated growth, first because interest rates tend to be much higher than available domestically and second because monies can often be compounded tax-free.

Also consider that assets left in the United States are particularly vulnerable to public disclosure and consequent loss. American bank records are anything but secure. Predators intent on sharing the wealth invariably go after those with the largest estates. As a consequence, a growing number of the wealthiest Americans — those in the entertainment world, for example — not only send their cash offshore but they move their residences overseas at the same time. Many of them choose to lease rather than buy residences in the U.S. for fear that visible tangible assets will attract litigious predators. They instead buy expensive real estate abroad where their properties are safe out of the reach of U.S. courts, creditors, and tax authorities.

If this scares you as it should, you would do well to consider offshore alternatives. The term *offshore* is broadly defined to mean outside your own nation's boundaries. What follows is a discussion of some of the most useful techniques available today.

Chapter Two

Advantages of Offshore Investing

Foreign investment provides several major benefits for Americans. Although our major concern here is privacy, savvy investors must also be concerned with investment safety, the potential for long-term growth, and cash liquidity. The same principles which apply to domestic investing also apply to investments made overseas. Unless you have money to burn, you wouldn't buy shares of stock or units of participation in an investment trust hawked by an overly aggressive salesperson working out of a Las Vegas telephone boiler room. Change the picture, putting the salesman in Paris or Frankfurt or Geneva and the cautions remain the same.

On the other hand, there is no inherent reason why you *shouldn't* consider investing abroad. Although laws and customs vary widely from nation to nation, the same rules., principles and practices apply to investments made in American and foreign institutions. When buying equity issues, for example, corporations with low capitalization are likely to offer the opportunity for greater long-term growth but at higher risk of loss. Volatility is a two-edged sword. For fixed-interest securities, specifically bonds, the same guidelines apply to both American and overseas instruments. The highest interest rates are offered by securities which are inherently more risky, which bear maturity dates further into the future, or which have poor secondary markets in which they can be sold short of maturity. Your first order of business is to decide on your objectives and the level of risk you are willing to undertake.

Stocks, Bonds, And Mutual Funds

Mutual funds which assemble portfolios of stocks, bonds, and other monetary instruments are common in both the United States and foreign markets. Again, the practices are surprisingly similar. Funds are often established to achieve specific objectives such as growth, income, a combination of growth and income, or capital preservation. Your own financial objectives coupled with your tolerance for risk will dictate which funds you should consider and which ones you should avoid, regardless of whether they are based in the United States or elsewhere. Investing in sector funds such as precious metals or banking or chemicals offers opportunities for greater capital appreciation than more balanced funds but they are also more risky because they are less diversified. Entire sectors can decline precipitously.

In short, everything you already know about investing in stocks, bonds, and mutual funds is largely applicable to the world markets. You want to avoid anything which looks too good to be true. It is also imperative that you work with well-established and respected securities brokers and advisors, just as you would at home.

None of this should come as a surprise because we live in a world characterized by a global economy. What happens on the New York Stock Exchange when the opening bell sounds is often the result of what has happened in Tokyo or London a few hours earlier and vice versa. Names like Xerox, McDonalds, Ford, and Mitsubishi are truly global. These multinationals manufacture and market their products worldwide, blurring national boundaries. They also attract investors from around the globe. With the passage of two important trade barrier-busting treaties (NAFTA and GATT) in recent years and the movement towards a common European currency, international investment will take on totally new dimensions.

Americans are often misled into making purchase as well as investment decisions on the basis of a "Buy American" fever. Patriotic as it may sound, it is virtually impossible in today's economy to buy goods of strictly American manufacture. Autos with American nameplates invariably contain parts, components, even entire assemblies or engines manufactured overseas. Today there are virtually no radios or televisions manufactured in the United States. In fact many economists predict that heavy manufacturing in the United States will continue to decline rapidly as other nations pick up the business. It may be that America is simply not as well suited as other nations to manufacturing by virtue of its labor costs and low productivity.

Sophisticated investors already know the importance of portfolio diversification. Some investment instruments do better in times of economic growth; others have historically performed better in periods of economic stagnation or uncertainty. Certain investments are most suited to long-term performance while others provide better liquidity in the short run. Depending on individual needs, preferences, and risk tolerance, investors often develop portfolios containing stocks, bonds, real estate investments, precious metals, cash, and cash equivalents.

Foreign securities, with the exception of mutual funds, can generally be bought and sold through any registered stock broker. Naturally, it is better to work with a broker who specializes in and understands foreign securities. Transactions will be expedited more quickly, commissions may be lower, and better research may lead you to better performing securities.

Mutual funds are particularly attractive for those who do not have the time or expertise to track and select individual securities for purchase or sale. The mutual fund's manager performs these functions, hopefully making prudent and timely decisions. Investing in mutual funds also allows you to diversify your portfolio much more broadly than you could ever do yourself. Many funds, those whose managers are free to buy and sell securities on a daily basis in response to changes in the markets, invest in hundreds of different underlying issues at any given moment. Some funds invest solely in stocks, others only in bonds, and still others in combinations of stocks, bonds, derivatives, or cash.

Investing in offshore funds offers all the advantages of fund diversification and expert management oversight coupled with asset protection against lawsuits, forfeitures, and the possibility of currency exchange controls in the future. An important distinction must be made, however, between investing in international funds that are American based and investing directly in offshore-based funds. Investments made in U.S. funds which purchase global securities provide opportunities for growth and diversification, but they fail to offer the kinds of protection against creditors and seizures only available through direct offshore investment.

Americans are not legally barred from buying offshore mutual funds although American brokers in many cases cannot make the trades. This is true only because many of these funds have not been registered with the Securities and Exchange Commission for sale in this country. Their lack of U.S. registration should not be construed to mean that these funds or unit trusts are in any way defective. On the contrary, thousands of offshore funds offer the highest levels of management expertise and financial performance. Many offshore fund operators simply choose not to register their products in the United States because they already have well-established markets overseas. Registration, which is quite costly, merely diminishes fund profitability. It would be imprudent to reduce financial returns for global investors just to satisfy the needs of a few American investors.

In addition, some offshore funds compensate their managers in a way significantly different from the traditional American model. American fund managers typically receive a fixed percentage of the fund's assets as compensation for their work. The amount can vary from 0.15% to 1.0% or more. Many progressive offshore funds use performance-based criteria instead. Fund managers are rewarded only when they successfully generate profits for their customers by buying and selling the right securities at the right time. Ironically, such performance-based compensation prevent these funds from being registered in the United States, where federal securities laws prohibit paying managers based on results.

Although it is perfectly legal for Americans to invest in unregistered offshore funds, it is illegal for such fund issuers to sell unregistered securities in the United States. Foreign securities issues unwilling to become entangled in the web of American bureaucracy often choose to play it completely safe, refusing to sell their funds to Americans even when they are living abroad.

To accomplish this, they sometimes require that fund purchasers sign a statement declaring that they are not citizens or residents of the United States.

There are several ways for Americans to circumvent this problem. The most obvious is to use a foreign mail forwarding service, filing a false declaration with the fund issuer. Although this is not likely to result in any problems, nobody having been defrauded of any money, a foreign government could conceivably take the position that an intentionally false declaration deserves punishment. If they were to follow the American lead on matters like this, the securities could be confiscated. Indeed the U.S. Department of Justice could argue that mail fraud was perpetrated by filing a false declaration of citizenship. Even if the commission of a crime could not be proved, the government could move towards civil forfeiture of the securities.

Two far better options for the acquisition of unregistered foreign securities are available. In the first case, a foreign bank or trust company is appointed as a nominee holder. The financial institution holds the security under an agreement for the true owner. The investor needs to make certain that the offshore fund does not require a statement indicating that the *beneficial owner* is not an American. Most funds do not require any such declaration.

Investors can add a second firewall to afford further protection. A foreign bank or trust company is appointed as trustee. The American investor remains the primary beneficiary with his spouse or children listed as contingent beneficiaries in case of death. The trust now becomes both the legal and beneficial owner of the securities. Although the trust now has American beneficiaries, the shares contained within the trust are not themselves beneficially owned by Americans.

These kind of trusts can be set up for about $500 in countries like Canada, Great Britain, and Hong Kong. In most cases, no withholding taxes will be payable when both the assets and beneficiaries are foreign. For purposes of tax credits in those situations where withholding taxes are taken from trust earnings, the Internal Revenue Service will only recognize common law trusts. Although Swiss banks can serve as trustees as well as nominees, the IRS might refuse to recognize such trusts for purposes of tax credits. Be certain that your trust qualifies as a common law trust, *not* a civil law trust. Forming a foreign trust is definitely a subject in which you want to be guided by professional legal and accounting advisors.

Higher Yields, Tax Benefits

Whatever the reasons may be for this domestic decline, you should not be intimidated into letting your money remain in relatively low-yielding local investments when far more attractive international opportunities abound. Investing overseas, particularly in emerging and rapidly expanding markets, provides avenues for diversification, growth, and often lower risk. Given the intricate nature of multinational business, investing overseas actually creates jobs in the United States — jobs in importing, transportation, accounting, packaging, marketing, even retailing.

There are also some significant tax advantages to investing offshore. Just as many states offer incentives to investors, encouraging them to build new plants in their jurisdictions with promises of tax relief or other subsidies, foreign governments sometimes offer incentives to attract capital to their growing economies. Americans can often take advantage of these situations, obtaining tax relief while safely investing overseas.

Domestic American incentives by contrast are few and far between. At one time, municipal bonds were attractive to high tax bracket investors because their interest was generally not taxable for purposes of federal income tax reporting. Unfortunately, bonds issued by American cities and towns to finance ventures like water treatment plans and nursing homes yield such low rates, often in the range of 3.0%, that they no longer keep pace with inflation. A bond which offers a 3.0% tax-free return, for example, is only equivalent to a yield of 4.35% from a taxable bond for a taxpayer in the 31 percent tax bracket. What's worse, we cannot rely on our cities and towns to remain solvent. Moody's, as well as Standard and Poors, the two most respected bond-rating services, have significantly downgraded their opinion of many American municipalities. .Several defaults and near-defaults have occurred in recent years and more are likely in the future as Washington shifts the expensive burden of providing social services to states and municipalities.

While many Individuals have been reticent about taking their assets offshore, American businesses have moved their operations overseas at a feverish pace. Walk through the streets of London, Paris, Zurich, Bonn, or even Moscow and you will recognize names like McDonalds, American Express, IBM, Xerox, and Avis everywhere. In some cases, the motivation to invest offshore was simply a case of expanding consumer markets. In other situations, large corporations chose to move assets abroad in search of lower taxes. For still others, overseas operations were seen as a means to counterbalance the uncertainties of economic downturns in the parent country. Individual investors can avail themselves of the same benefits that major American corporations find in offshore opportunities.

If It Seems Too Good To Be True

In selecting offshore alternatives, you need to stay away from all the same pitfalls that plague domestic investors. Social unrest or upheaval can play havoc anywhere in the world. If you were an investor in a small business in Los Angeles, one that was burned to the ground during the riots of 1982, you would probably have learned a lesson about investing in tinderboxes. A quick reading of the pages of the *New York Times* or the *Wall Street Journal* will clearly identify global hot spots fraught with uncertainty. Despite strides towards peace, lingering problems in the Middle East, Northern Ireland, and parts of Africa might give you reason to pause before investing heavily in these regions. It may be too early to say whether the climate in the republics formed by the breakup of the old Soviet Union are sufficiently stable for American investment. Fortunately there are numerous stable governments where investments are at least as safe as those made in the United States, and perhaps safer.

Investing offshore offers three big advantages over investing domestically. First, there are opportunities for more rapid wealth accumulation. Interest rates are often substantially higher abroad, equity investments in many developing and emerging markets provide good opportunities for upside movement, and you may also benefit from currency fluctuations if you are an astute investor. American banks are saddled with the heavy burdens of regulation. By some estimates, bank profits are reduced by as much as 20 percent just to maintain compliance with the myriad of rules.

The Federal Reserve System, America's central bank, siphons off a substantial portion of every member bank's deposits, keeping it in reserve but without interest. One might think this is done for safety purposes when in fact it is done to manipulate the money supply and to control the level of domestic inflation. Other federal regulations actually require banks to make unsound loans, to invest in dubious businesses or economically hard-pressed areas where loan defaults are sure to cause losses. The paperwork itself is monumental, causing American banks and thrift institutions to pad their payrolls with thousands of otherwise unnecessary accountants, auditors, attorneys, and compliance officers.

Who pays for all of this regulation? The individual or corporate investor does. In order to maintain adequate spreads, i.e. the difference between interest earned on outstanding loans and interest paid on savings to their depositors, American banks are forced to do two things. First, they must pay substandard interest to their depositors, often a fraction of the rates paid offshore. Secondly, they must charge exorbitant interest rates to borrowers. Even so, the American banking community's profits have been wobbly at best, many institutions having faced serious losses for successive years, some of them having failed completely.

Avoiding Witch Hunts

A second good reason for considering offshore investments is secrecy. There are simply no mechanisms in the United States for protecting your privacy. Federal, state, and local governments can examine your portfolios at will under the guise of tax compliance or law enforcement. In many cases, these examinations are random and not even brought about by any suspicion of tax evasion or the commission of any crime.

The Internal Revenue Service has for years conducted Taxpayer Compliance Audits, the most arbitrary and oppressive of all its audits. The ostensible purpose was to collect statistical information to help it determine which classes of taxpayers were complying with the tax codes and which ones were not. For the individual taxpayer subjected to one of these witch-hunts, the audit becomes anything but a statistical examination.

The usual presumption of innocence which Americans have come to believe protects them is not compatible with IRS philosophy or practices. A person subjected to a Taxpayer Compliance Audit is required to prove every aspect of his life. If he claims on the return to be married, he will be asked to provide a marriage certificate. If he claims dependents, he will be compelled to provide birth certificates. The taxpayer may be asked to produce bank statements, stock and bond transaction confirmations, and any other financial records the auditor deems useful. Of course the IRS will already be in receipt of all kinds of information on your financial dealings as a result of various Form 1099's that have been filed by banks, mortgagors, and other payers of interest and dividends. Any taxpayer who is unable to produce the requested records may find his deductions and exemptions disallowed. The IRS may even attempt to ascribe to the taxpayer income that did not exist.

Even if you aren't called in for a dreaded Taxpayer Compliance Audit, there is still a good chance you will be subjected to a much more widely-applied audit process after your tax return is *scored* by IRS computers.

The reported values for earned income, interest and dividends earned, business deductions, charitable contributions, taxes and interest paid, casualty losses, and other line items are compared to national norms. The more your return differs from established averages, the higher the score it receives. The highest scored returns are then examined by auditors.

Should a dispute arise, you may be forced to take the matter to Tax Court, a special judicial body authorized by Congress. Despite all the rhetoric about a Taxpayer Bill of Rights, the current IRS system and its puppet Tax Court are far from impartial in deciding tax cases. Indeed, in order to take your grievance before Tax Court, you will be required to pay all the monies, interest, and penalties the government *says* you owe and then, in effect, sue Uncle Sam for its return. You probably have a better chance waiting for Ed McMahon to deliver the winning prize from American Family Publishers.

Asset Preservation

The third and most compelling reason for keeping funds offshore is asset preservation. Many Americans are lulled into believing that deposits in American banks provide the ultimate protection against loss. After all, the Federal Deposit Insurance Corporation (FDIC) insures each individual depositor up to $100,000 at each bank in which he or she maintains an account. This has proven to be satisfactory in cases where small rural banks fail. What would happen, however, if a rush on banks caused the largest American institutions like Chase or Citibank to start failing one after another?

Consider what happened to the Federal Savings and Loan Insurance Corporation (FSLIC) when savings and loan associations started tumbling like dominos. You don't see those initials anymore because this government insurer is now defunct, the FDIC having taken jurisdiction over thrifts as well as commercial banks. The Resolution Trust Corporation, a federal government-sanctioned agency, moved in to liquidate billions of dollars of nearly-worthless bank portfolios.

Thousands of depositors whose accounts exceeded FSLIC insurance limits lost millions of dollars. Many others who held high-interest certificates of deposit, certificates they thought were contractual obligations between themselves and their savings and loan associations, were stunned when their failed thrifts were sold. The institutions which took over the old deposits and CD's were not obliged to honor the contracted interest rates so they unilaterally established new ones. Investors who held ten-year CD's paying 10 percent interest suddenly found that they were holding certificates unilaterally renegotiated to 4 percent.

If a major bank failure were to occur in the United States, and some forecasters say it is inevitable, the FDIC would be powerless to protect customers. The FDIC trust maintains less than a penny for every insured dollar. Foreign depositories, despite lack of such illusory insurance schemes, often provide better protection against bank failures because they can operate profitably in the absence of restrictive government regulations.

In most cases, offshore banks are also immune from oppressive government taxes. Governments are happy to allow them to operate free from such burdens knowing that the potential for higher profitability will ultimately attract more foreign money. In the United States, by contrast, federal and state governments look first to the banks for taxation and then a second time to depositors who earn interest from them.

The disparity of interest rates between American and other offshore banks has historically been very significant. When American banks were paying rates in the 4 percent range, European and Asian banks were offering 10 percent. Under this scenario, a $100,000 deposit would have earned $110,350 more over a ten-year period in an offshore bank with annual compounding. Add the potential benefits of lower taxes and the offshore depositor is a world ahead.

For most people with substantial assets, protection from private creditors is even more important than protection from government intruders or massive bank failures. In a litigious society like ours, causes of action resulting in large judgments are numerous. You can be successfully sued for breach of contract, defamation, negligence resulting in physical or emotional injury, discrimination, product liability, wrongful death, and a host of others. Jurors have no qualms about awarding inappropriately high judgments since they are playing with other people's funds. Judges, bowing to political pressures and the prospect of eventual reelection, rarely set aside or modify such awards, ridiculous as they might seem.

By keeping funds safely tucked away offshore, creditors will find it difficult if not impossible to locate your assets. Even if you are ordered by a court to produce certified copies of tax returns which disclose the existence of offshore bank accounts, your adversaries would have to file separate court actions overseas to obtain judgments against you. This can take many years, giving you the opportunity to hold your creditors at bay while you appeal the judgment. This is important because once your assets have been seized and turned over to creditors, there is no guarantee that you would ever be able to retrieve them even if an appeal court later reversed the judgment.

Unless a Draconian court order is issued preventing you from accessing your own offshore assets in the meantime, you may have the opportunity to transfer them again, thwarting your creditors with an elaborate shell game. Certain offshore accounts can be set up in a manner which further protects them from seizure, allowing you to legally transfer your assets to dependents and out of the grips of potential creditors. The Swiss annuity, discussed in the next chapter, is such an example.

Paper Trails And Requirements

Most transactions involving checks, money orders, and wire transfers leave indelible paper trails. This is important to note in setting up foreign bank accounts because a visible trail can negate some of the benefits of having a secret account overseas. Accounts can be set up in person or by mail. Some foreign banks actually require initial personal visits in order to get acquainted with their new customers. In either case, the question remains — how will you transfer your assets overseas?

American law requires you to report, via IRS Form 4789 or U.S. Customs Service Form 4790, the movement of more than $10,000 in cash or equivalents in or out of the country. The law is applicable to traveler's checks, bearer bonds, and other negotiable securities as well as cash movements. U.S. banks which transfer funds overseas on your behalf are required to file directly with the government. You cannot simply divide a large chunk of money into smaller pieces under $10,000 to avoid reporting. Under current law, this would constitute money laundering, subjecting you to a prison sentence as long as 20 years, hefty fines, and forfeiture of your assets.

Of course a family of five can legally move as much as $50,000 in cash or equivalents across national borders without worrying about filing requirements; the assets for each family member should be kept below $10,000 and moved separately. Because the U.S. Banking Secrecy Act also requires individuals to report their ownership of foreign bank accounts valued at $10,000 or more, large families can consider establishing separate accounts for each of their family members. The value of accounts will of course depend on exchange rates between the U.S. dollar and the particular denominated currency in which the account is kept. For purposes of compliance with U.S. law, the official exchange rate calculated by the Federal Reserve Bank of New York must be known. Unfortunately, these rates are not released until the end of the calendar year. If you then learn that your accounts have exceeded the limitation at any time during the preceding year, you will be required to disclose their existence. For safety sake, you should keep your account values far enough below the $10,000 thresholds to allow for both currency fluctuations and the accumulation of interest, if any.

Another practical method to avoid reaching the $10,000 limit is to buy foreign stocks or bonds overseas with any excess cash you may have available. It is important to take delivery of the instrument in your name, although it can be left in a safe deposit box or with a banker offshore. The key is to make certain the certificate needs your personal endorsement to be sold or negotiated. Stocks or bonds held in securities or brokerage accounts on your behalf do not provide an exemption from reporting requirements. These assets must be totalled with the cash in your offshore bank accounts to determine whether you exceed the $10,000 reporting limitation. Mutual funds, because they are generally held in securities accounts, cannot be used in this same fashion unless they are issued as certificates registered in your name. Be certain you understand this distinction. You can also consider direct investments in real estate, annuities or personal property offshore, none of which are subject to the $10,000 account reporting limitation. Many Americans have made direct investments in gems, precious metals, even antique cars.

When all is said and done, however, the magic $10,000 limitations imposed by American law on reporting offshore bank and brokerage accounts or cash transactions are not nearly the impediments they might seem — unless absolute secrecy is desired. For most serious investors with substantial assets, moving money offshore still makes sense despite these reporting requirements. Even if you have to disclose to Uncle Sam that you have moved money abroad, the assets will still be protected against attachment by American courts. Furthermore, the status of your wealth will not routinely show up in the myriad of American databases maintained not only by government agencies but by credit bureaus and other private-sector eavesdroppers. In addition, many exceptional offshore vehicles are available for managing assets — vehicles which are *not* subject to the reporting requirements of U.S. authorities. We will discuss these in later chapters.

In short, reporting requirements can often be viewed more as nuisances than serious obstacles to the private, secure, offshore management of assets. Even if you have to report the export of cash or other negotiable securities, the government need not know where the money is ultimately parked, particularly if you make use of the kinds of asset protection trusts and companies we will discuss later. The use of *qualified* offshore advisors is a key ingredient to meeting your objectives. Properly done, many types of structures can be created that need not be reported at all. A Congressional study estimated that in 1995 alone, $430 billion went into offshore asset protection trusts. So obviously a lot of people are concentrating on diversification and protection, rather than worry about absolute secrecy.

Another issue needs discussion at this time. Americans are paying an ever-increasing number of bills electronically. In most communities, it is possible to pay your electric, phone, gas, and cable bills automatically each month by electronic funds transfer. Some mortgagees take their payments this way, too. If you are employed by a large company, there is a good chance that your earnings are directly deposited into your checking account. The Internal Revenue Service which has for several years encouraged taxpayers to claim their refunds by direct deposit may one day stop issuing printed checks altogether. Nearly 20 million Americans now file their individual income tax returns electronically, making IRS audits twice as easy as before.

If you pay for your groceries with a Visa debit card or one issued by a similar bank card company, you have left yet another paper trail. Remember that in the eyes of the Internal Revenue Service, you have to prove yourself innocent if you are called in for an audit. If you start making purchases which seemingly exceed your earnings, you may have some serious explaining to do.

Offshore Investing Makes Sense

Offshore banking does *not* eliminate U.S. taxes on your earnings. Americans are required to pay federal income tax on all earnings, domestic and foreign. To do otherwise could subject you to prosecution for tax evasion.

Nonetheless it is widely recognized that hundreds of millions of dollars in offshore earnings goes unreported. The IRS estimates that more than $100 billion in annual revenue falls between the chairs despite its $5 billion operating budget and more than 120,000 employees. Since the 1990, almost $15 billion has been appropriated by Congress for additional computer capacity and modernization. The more Congress throws money at the IRS, the wider the gap gets between expected and actual tax receipts.

Many nations have entered into double-taxation treaties with the United States. These allow Americans to take a credit on their U.S. federal tax returns for interest income already subjected to tax by foreign governments. The account holder sacrifices privacy, however, by taking advantage of such arrangements because he has to disclose the existence of his overseas accounts.

Privacy is best maintained when transactions involve cash. If you maintain offshore accounts in places that you periodically visit, cash deposits and withdrawals or those made with traveler's checks yield the highest levels of security. Deposits made by personal checks drawn on out-of-state accounts provide better shields than bank checks or wires. Some overseas banks also issue bank cards such as VISA which allow you to debit your foreign accounts directly. These transactions clear offshore, out of the prying eyes of U.S. officials.

Consider what the future is likely to bring before you make a decision about offshore investing. Look at the political as well as economic climate. By Congressional Budget Office estimates, there will be one retired American collecting Social Security for every two working contributors by the year 2020. The retirement fund will be dead broke long before that time if taxes aren't raised or benefits drastically reduced, the latter a political impossibility. Americans in 1997 paid payroll taxes for Social Security equivalent to 6.20 percent of their earnings up to $65,400 and an additional 1.45 percent for Medicare with no limit on earnings. Bear in mind that employers matched those amounts; self-employed people picked up both portions less a small tax credit.

Another way to look at the fiscal crisis is to examine the Social Security Administration's total projected obligations and its forecasted tax receipts. When converted to *present values*, i.e. adjusted for the effects of inflation, a deficit of nearly $1.4 trillion emerges. The bubble has got to burst sooner or later.

Two major consequences should be considered. First, the pension you thought you earned may not be there at all. Today there is an earnings test for Social Security recipients who continue to work past retirement age. Tomorrow there may be an assets test. Those who were smart enough to invest wisely for their retirement years may also be precluded from collecting benefits.

These frightening facts of life exist before you even consider the effects of federal income taxes, state and local income taxes, sales taxes, personal property taxes, and a myriad of other taxes governments concoct. No wonder politicians are afraid to talk about *tax increases*, preferring instead to invent euphemisms like *revenue enhancers* to describe the way they take your money.

The second consequence of government insolvency could be catastrophic economic collapse. The dollar, once heralded as the international standard for currency exchange purposes, could fall into further disrepute. Since the end of World War II, the U.S. dollar has declined precipitously in value, particularly in relation to gold. By 1997 it had lost 95 percent of its value. As the United States started printing more and more currency, none of it backed by gold reserves, things got worse.

A good hedge against the possibility of the dollar's collapse makes sense now more than ever before. Maintaining a portion of your portfolio in an array of strong foreign currencies like the Swiss franc can protect you in the event the dollar precipitously loses value

In an effort to get out of the grips of government thieves, many people started hoarding money. A lot of it went underground. Nobody knows with certainty how large the American *underground economy* is, but it is certainly massive — valued at billions of dollars. It includes many legitimate businesses which simply fail to report or grossly under-report income, the effect of unreported barter transactions, and of course criminal activity.

In an effort to flush out some of this money so that it can start collecting taxes on it, government considered all kinds of novel approaches. The Reagan administration sent out a trial balloon for consideration, suggesting a nationwide currency recall. Under the proposal, all large-denomination paper currency would have been reissued in a new form. Americans would have been given a limited period, perhaps as little as two weeks, to convert all old notes into new ones. Those who failed to do so would be left holding worthless currency. Of course the Internal Revenue Service would have geared up to question individuals with large sums of cash. More than likely, those unable to prove that the bills did not represent the proceeds of crime or drug dealing would have had their money confiscated. The proposal was too bold and it failed, at least for the time being.

Other proposals, seemingly less intrusive but nonetheless dangerous, remain on the drawing board. One suggests that all currency be bar-coded so that serial numbers can be easily read by scanners. The far-reaching effect of such currency would be to create an insidious paper trail for virtually all financial and commercial transactions. With the advent of what many people have termed the *cashless society*, governments may find that their dream is coming true.

The decision to move assets offshore should be made not only in light of privacy problems that already exist but with an eye towards what the future may bring. Offshore investments make a lot of sense for honest Americans concerned about the safety and security of their holdings.

Chapter Three

The Swiss Connection

Most Americans think of Switzerland, especially when they factor *privacy* into the investment equation. The Swiss franc has maintained stability better than any other currency. Moreover, unlike the American dollar which is only partially backed by gold reserves, Washington believing that the "full faith and credit of the United States" is sufficient backing, every Swiss franc is backed by close to 150% of its value in gold reserves. Switzerland has maintained its neutrality through two world wars and numerous other regional conflicts. It has therefore not suffered the economic consequences that others have sustained. In many respects, the Swiss enjoy democratic traditions that far surpass those in America, a national referendum process insuring that Swiss citizens directly determine national policy.

Traditional Swiss bank accounts have been popular for all these reasons and others. Interest rates have been modest at best and earnings by foreigners have long been subject to a 35% withholding tax. Why then, one might ask, would American investors deposit hundreds of millions of dollars in Swiss banks? One reason is that the Swiss franc has markedly appreciated against the U.S. dollar over a ten-year period, partially offsetting the cost of withholding taxes. Fiscal and monetary responsibility by governments apparently pay dividends.

Swiss Law And Bank Secrecy

A second and perhaps more important attraction for American investors is Swiss law which protects financial privacy. For many centuries, Switzerland maintained an environment in which its people could bank in complete security, out of sight from the prying eyes of other individuals or even government officials. Naturally, this attracted worldwide attention and huge sums of money began to flow into Swiss banks for safekeeping. It wasn't until 1934 and the rise of the Nazis in Germany, however, that the Swiss government actually embodied the heritage of banking privacy into law. The immediate reason was to protect Germans who had sent money out of the country to Switzerland to protect it against impending disaster; the German government had made it illegal for its nationals to maintain foreign bank accounts.

Under normal conditions, Swiss government and bank employees are forbidden from disclosing any information about bank accounts. It is unlawful for them to even confirm the mere existence of an account in the name of a particular individual. Enforcement is vigorous with hefty fines and prison sentences meted out to violators. Additionally, such disclosures can be prosecuted under Article 28 of the Swiss Civil Code, allowing injured victims to successfully recover monetary damages from banks and their employees.

Customers can of course ask their Swiss bankers to release information as in the case of requests for credit references. The banks cannot otherwise release information, however, unless ordered to do so by Swiss courts. Those who ask their banks to disclose account information as a result of a foreign court order may be considered to be acting under duress, allowing the bank for refuse such requests.

It must be pointed out, however, that the Swiss system is not without loopholes. Bowing to pressures of other nations faced with tax enforcement problems, Swiss bank privacy has been largely eroded in recent years. As a result of international treaties signed by Switzerland, the United States, and other developed countries, account information can be released when deposited monies are in some way related to crimes committed in other countries. The alleged crimes must also be criminal offenses in Switzerland.

These treaties have only muddied the water because tax evasion is considered a civil matter in Switzerland, not a criminal offense. Nonetheless, allegations of tax evasion by American officials are often accompanied by real or fabricated allegations of other criminal activities such as drug dealing, organized crime, or money laundering. The latter, now considered a crime in Switzerland, has put a new face on Swiss banking laws.

Under Swiss law, assets are presumed to be controlled by criminal organizations when they result from the commission of crimes and are therefore subject to forfeiture under the criminal code. Such asset seizures require a Court Order of Forfeiture. The order can be appealed by the defendant or his bank. In either case, the appellant would have to show that the assets in question were not linked to criminal activity or that the amount was disproportionate to the gain actually incurred. Under articles 58 and 59 of the Swiss Criminal Code, however, the assets or bank deposits may still be frozen by the government during the appeal process.

The Strasbourg Convention (ratified by Switzerland in 1992) as well as the UN Convention against Drug Trafficking (1988) imposed new rules on Switzerland and others, requiring domestic confiscation procedures. Moreover, these treaties imposed obligations on each signatory state to confiscate the proceeds of crimes requested by other states who also signed on to these treaties. Assets transferred to innocent third parties also became the targets of seizure although a number of exceptions were included to prevent severe hardships.

In 1996, the Swiss government allowed the Cantons of Zurich and Vaud to share more than $175 million frozen in 1994. The money had been deposited by a Colombian citizen in a couple of dozen accounts at a major Zurich bank. Swiss courts determined that the assets had resulted from criminal drug trafficking and accordingly seized them.

In 1995, Swiss authorities froze more than $100 million in bank deposits which they believed were made by Paul Salinas, brother of Mexico's former president, Carlos Salinas. Swiss police then arrested Salinas' wife and her brother when they tried to make withdrawals from the Geneva bank. The accounts all bore fictitious names. The United States Drug

Enforcement Administration had tipped off Swiss officials that the assets allegedly resulted from money laundering and narcotics trafficking.

Coming to the aid of Salinas was Carlos Peralta, a well-respected businessman heavily involved in the cellular phone industry. He insisted that he gave Salinas $50 million to invest in a capital venture fund and that as many as 20 other prominent Mexican businessmen had similarly funded the investment. The moral to the story is that *guilty until proven innocent* is no longer a strictly American philosophy. The DEA, IRS, and other American institutions have extended their tentacles to the far-reaching corners of the earth.

Drug trafficking and money laundering are not the only crimes which could lead to account disclosures or asset forfeitures. Switzerland has also made insider trading a criminal offense and has since cooperated with the United States and others in sharing information in this connection. In a recent case which eventually reached Switzerland's Federal Tribunal (its Supreme Court), judges affirmed the right of France's Stock Exchange Commission to obtain assistance from Swiss authorities in a case involving insider trading.

The litigation arose from a stock purchase in which a Geneva-based buyer acquired a block of stock in a French company just days before another group took control of a still larger stake. The French suspected insider trading violations. The purchaser demanded that his name not be disclosed, arguing that the French Stock Exchange Commission had no powers to dole out penalties in France and thus could not proceed under the terms of any international treaty. The decision of the court effectively broadened the powers of foreign administrative bodies to successfully collect information from their Swiss counterparts. Such information, however, cannot later be used as evidence in criminal prosecutions.

As a practical matter then, Swiss financial institutions no longer offer the ultimate protection in financial privacy that once attracted millions of investors, savory and unsavory alike. Like the anonymous Swiss numbered bank account which is now a thing of the past, many earlier privacy protections have crumpled under the weight of international pressure.

By signing on in 1995 to the Hague Convention on the Service Abroad of Judicial and Extra Judicial Documents as well as the Hague Convention on Taking of Evidence Abroad in Civil and Commercial Matters, Switzerland opened its doors to international mutual assistance in civil matters. To effect such assistance in criminal matters, the Swiss joined the Mutual Assistance, the Transfer of Sentenced Persons, and the Laundering, Search, Seizure and Confiscation of the Proceeds from Crime treaties. It has entered into special bilateral agreements with the United States, Canada, Australia, Japan, and Russia.

The Swiss Federal Act on International Assistance in Criminal Matters puts some limitations on the role Swiss institutions can play in international requests for assistance. Courts will only compel the release of information when a crime, punishable in both countries, is under investigation. The information requested will only be furnished when direct relevance is established and then only in proportion to the proof required. Even when information is furnished, it can only be used in connection with the agreed criminal proceedings. Foreign governments cannot use the same information to prosecute other administrative, fiscal, tax, political, or military matters.

Despite these trends, a public referendum in 1984 affirmed by a very wide margin the Swiss people's desire to maintain bank secrecy. The Swiss Parliament specifically exempted tax evasion cases from international judicial assistance although tax fraud cases are still subject to information disclosure among treaty members.

Banking has been a major Swiss enterprise and any further erosion in laws which protect privacy will surely cause money to pour out of its economy into more favorable repositories. Switzerland still provides levels of bank secrecy and financial security that are uncommon in other nations including the United States. Those not involved in criminal activity can continue to benefit from Swiss banking practices. For the average person, bank secrecy in Switzerland is more than sufficient.

Banks in Switzerland are tightly regulated by the Banking Commission, facing comprehensive periodic audits. In addition, capital requirements far exceed those required in most countries of the world including the United States. Historians know that the Great Crash of 1929 was largely brought about by massive runs on American banks, depositors lining up at their banks to close their accounts in the face of impending economic disaster. Of course, the banks had little or no liquidity and collapsed, leaving millions of depositors penniless.

It is true that we have a Federal Reserve System today which regulates capital and liquidity requirements. We also have agencies such as the Federal Deposit Insurance Corporation (FDIC) which purportedly guarantees our deposits, at least up to $100,000 per depositor per bank. Many observers are skeptical, however, that FDIC would be able to pay its obligations in the event of another national banking collapse. Recent events in both the banking and thrift institution communities suggest that a full-fledged banking system collapse in the United States may not be that far-fetched despite the reforms instituted since the Great Depression.

Additionally, Swiss accounting principles are more in tune with reality than those in the United States. Swiss banks are required to maintain 7% to 9% of their liabilities in hard equities. Securities which they own must be valued monthly at cost or market value, whichever is less, preventing the accumulation of large portfolios of *unrealized losses*. Remember how Americans were stunned when savings and loan associations began to fold like paper fans. Their portfolios included billions of dollars in bad real estate investments, loans which were effectively concealed from depositors and stockholders for years until the collapses became imminent.

Chapter Three

Full-service Banking: Savings And Investments

One other unusual characteristic of Swiss banking is that it is broad-based. American financial institutions and those of most other countries tend to specialize in one of two areas: banking *or* investment. The separation of the two functions in the United States was largely predicated on American banking law which, until recently, precluded banks from selling investment products like stocks, bonds, mutual funds, or real estate investment trusts. When this prohibition was lifted, Washington was plagued again with all sorts of problems. Many depositors, totally unaccustomed to investing at all, erroneously thought that mutual funds bought through American banks were FDIC insured. Washington had to issue new disclosure requirements for banks dealing in such sales.

Some American banks are now trying to do what the Swiss have done for generations. First Union, an American giant in the banking business, began a media blitz in which it talked of two trains, one which served only the east coast, the other the west. Its television spots show the tracks being joined, one train now providing both banking and investment services nationally. Unfortunately, this trend in American banking may be too little, too late. American banks have little experience on the investment side and federal regulations still stymie the delivery of a full range of services. It is also important to note that Swiss banks have maintained branches for years in major financial capitals such as New York, London, and Tokyo.

More significant, however, is the continuing issue of *privacy,* something that simply cannot be provided by American financial institutions on either the banking or investment sides. Privacy, coupled with an unsurpassed record of achievement in financial management, has drawn funds to Switzerland to the tune of two trillion dollars, half of the world's private portfolio business.

One of the leaders in Swiss financial management is JML Swiss Investment Counsellors, a firm which offers a unique style of financial management.

Clients can customize and control their own portfolios and still receive comprehensive management advice from some of the world's best experts on financial matters.

Recognizing that investors have differing goals, time frames, and tolerance for risk, JML's managers work with their individual clients to help them target their unique objectives. This naturally requires continued surveillance and analysis of worldwide economic trends, political events, financial markets, currencies, and other factors which could make some investments particularly attractive and others most unfavorable. Few individuals have the time or expertise to undertake this kind of evaluation themselves.

In any event, JML clumps the various opportunities that are available to investors into five separate categories for consideration by its Personal Portfolio Management Program clients:

*Cash Equivalents. Principal and interest are guaranteed, finite terms are provided, and yield potentials are typically above 5% per annum.

*Blue Chips. The investment portfolio consists of high-quality securities purchased for long-term capital appreciation potential. Expected yields are over 7%.

* Trading. The portfolio consists of securities which are bought and sold for short-term capital appreciation with potential return expected to exceed 10%.

* Trends. Often referred to a cyclical portfolios, securities are selected on the basis of economic forecasts by industry, sector, or country. The investor normally needs to wait about six years to realize annual returns exceeding 15%.

* Visions. The most speculative of the five categories, investments are selected from opportunities in emerging markets and new technologies. It may take ten or more years to realize average annual yields of 20% or more.

Further information about JML can be obtained by writing the following:

JML Jurg M. Lattmann AG
Swiss Investment Counsellors
Baarerstrasse 53, Department 212
CH-6304 Zug, Switzerland

Their telephone number is (41) 41 726 5500 and their fax number is (41) 41 726 5590, marking the fax to "Attention Department 212."

Potential American investors may also want to consider the expertise of Weber Hartmann Vrijhof & Partners, an independent portfolio management firm. The principals of this partnership, former bankers and portfolio managers, provide services to individuals, offshore trusts, and corporations in need of investment advice.

The minimum opening portfolio to be managed by this firm is $200,000 or equivalent. The management team here normally recommends that a portion of the portfolio be invested in hard currencies other than the U.S. dollar including the Swiss franc, French franc, German mark, and Dutch guilder. Respected for their conservative approach to portfolio management, the partners have recently invested heavily in short-term bonds and have achieved double-digit yields for their clients in 1995 and 1996.

As an independent asset management company, this firm and others like it profit when their clients make money since their compensation is calculated as a small percentage of the clients' assets under management. Unlike banks and brokerage houses which charge fees for transactions and thus benefit more from *churning* assets than making them grow, strong financial performance is the incentive for companies like Weber Hartmann Vrijhof & Partners.

For more information, you can write to the following:

Weber Hartmann Vrijhof & Partners Ltd.
Attn: New Clients Department
Zurichshstrasse 110B
8134 Adllswil, Switzerland

Their telephone number is (41-1) 709-11-15 and their fax number (41-1) 709-11-13, Attention New Clients Department.

Swiss Annuities

Of special interest to American investors are Swiss annuities. They are not subject to the 35% Swiss withholding tax on earned interest which is otherwise applicable to foreigners. These annuities, offered by Swiss insurance companies, are highly regulated by government authorities to insure adequate funding. Most importantly, the issuers are exempt from all reporting requirements, assuring that the anonymity of annuitants is preserved.

No government agency, Swiss or foreign, will ever receive information that a policy has been issued, that payments have been received, that interest or that dividends have been disbursed. The investor can choose to have his annuity payments paid annually, semiannually, or quarterly. The policies are denominated in Swiss francs, but distributions can be made in any other currency desired including U.S. dollars. Historically, Swiss annuities have paid yields equivalent to those of banks. They are arguably every bit as safe.

In many respects, the Swiss annuity looks and feels more like a savings account than an American-style deferred annuity. Management fees are small, usually less than half of one percent, and there is complete liquidity unlike American counterparts which often require penalties as high as seven percent of principal in the early years. A penalty of 500 Swiss francs and loss of accrued interest applies to liquidated accounts, regardless of size, but only during the annuity's first year. After one year, all principal, interest, and dividends are immediately available for liquidation.

Swiss annuities, unlike many American annuity and mutual fund products, are sold on a *no-load* basis, devoid of either up-front or sales redemption charges. By contrast, many mutual funds managed by the largest American issuers apply fees as high as five percent or more when purchasing or selling their products. Swiss annuities typically earn about the same rate of interest as long-term government bonds representative of the currency in which these annuities are issued. The investor thus gains the higher yields more often associated with long-term instruments and still maintains excellent shorter-term liquidity. Interest and dividend income are guaranteed by the insurance companies.

The investor can choose a lump sum distribution at maturity in which case capital gains taxes would be payable on the aggregate earnings. He can also roll the annuity over into an income annuity, deferring taxes until income is received at a later date, or he can extend the term of the annuity with its issuer, allowing him to continue deferring taxes until it is finally liquidated.

Another special feature of Swiss annuities is that they offer excellent protection against creditors. They cannot be attached by creditors if the purchaser has named his spouse or children as beneficiaries. An individual with substantial assets can therefore protect a portion of his portfolio against creditors by investing in Swiss annuities. Annuities are insurance policies under Swiss law and are immune from seizure by creditors. The only caveat is that the policy must have been purchased at least six months before bankruptcy proceedings or creditor collection procedures begin. This is designed to prevent individuals from fraudulently shielding monies against specific judgments.

Such annuities will not be seized by Swiss authorities even if ordered to do so by foreign courts. Policyholders can convert their revocable beneficiary annuities to irrevocable instruments in the case of bankruptcy. Under Swiss law, the beneficiaries then become the policyholders with full control over the annuities. The original annuitant no longer owns the policy, no longer has control, and cannot legally demand liquidation of the policy or repatriation of funds. When the beneficiaries notify the insurance company that a bankruptcy has occurred, the insurance company will ignore all requests or demands of the original annuitant to liquidate the policies.

The astute investor can thus shield his assets from creditors with fully revocable beneficiary designations. The change to irrevocable beneficiary designations need only be made if calamity strikes during the term of the annuity.

The choice of annuity payout options, incidentally, is made with the same considerations you would make for a conventional annuity issued in the United States. Your current age, life expectancy, and financial condition of your beneficiaries will determine what options best suit your needs. Straight life annuities, for example, continue to pay you for as long as you live, but your dependents receive nothing upon your death.

Annuities written *with refund* or for a particular number of *years certain* guarantee that if you should die early your designated beneficiaries will receive the accumulated funds or alternatively a specific number of periodic payments. The amount of the payment made monthly, quarterly, or annually of course depends on the option you have chosen, astute actuaries having calculated the probable payout the insurance company will make under these differing scenarios.

Swiss annuities may not be legally advertised or sold in the United States, but they are lawfully available for purchase by U.S. residents. In fact, they offer a special advantage for American citizens. Because it does not qualify as a foreign bank account, the Swiss annuity is not subject to the normal reporting requirements of Treasury Department forms used for reporting foreign bank accounts. Fund transfers by check or wire are also not reportable since they are not cash or cash equivalents as defined by government regulation.

Banking With Swiss Insurance Companies

Another interesting twist to Swiss law is a provision which allows Swiss insurance companies to offer foreign investors the opportunities to bank with them. Investors avail themselves of all the advantages of Swiss financial transactions including high yields, safety, stability, and secrecy. The *premium deposit account* with an insurance company, however, does not qualify as a bank account under American law. United States residents do not have to report the existence of such accounts under current law. The Swiss apply no withholding tax to these accounts and there is typically no ceiling on how much you can deposit. Even more comforting is the fact that premium deposit accounts normally pay higher yields than comparable bank accounts.

By maintaining a premium deposit account with the insurance company that holds your annuity, automatic premium payments can be made in a timely fashion. The most cost-effective practice is to make annual premium payments, avoiding the sometimes hefty surcharges imposed by insurance companies for semiannual, quarterly, or monthly premium payments. By avoiding the use of a Swiss bank account whose existence must be reported to U.S. authorities, privacy and anonymity can be maintained.

Premium deposit accounts cannot be used for purchasing gold, securities, or other investments. It is designed as an interest-bearing account strictly for the purpose of funding associated annuities. Nonetheless, such accounts provide a safe, private, and financially sound vehicle for savings.

One final benefit of dealing with Swiss insurance companies deserves mention, although some would argue that it may be far-fetched. The establishment of exchange controls by the United States is not out of the question in the foreseeable future. The government would not likely institute such controls unless it became desperate, but some observers believe that the ever-growing national debt may one day lead to such desperation. If history repeats itself, exchange controls would be accompanied by the forced repatriation of investments held overseas by Americans. Naturally, bank accounts would be included in such sweeping repatriations. It is probable that annuities and other arrangements with foreign insurance companies would not be covered by such drastic legislation since these represent pending contracts that have not yet been fulfilled.

Pension And Retirement Planning

Many Americans have discovered Swiss annuities and other foreign investment vehicles for pension and retirement plans. American law requires that assets held by such plans be under the physical control of trustees in the United States. Although the benefits of privacy are of course diminished when American trustees must be appointed, direct foreign investments still offer the advantages of exceptional growth, competitive yields, and protections inherent in holding assets denominated in foreign currencies.

Foreign currency certificates of deposit as well as Swiss annuities are well suited for retirement plans. These include Individual Retirement Arrangement (IRA) plans and Keogh accounts for the self-employed. Many Americans who opt for early retirement from companies with deferred compensation plans including 401-K and 403-B programs are faced with the dilemma of choosing appropriate investments for their distributions. Rollover and conduit IRA's may make use of foreign investment vehicles so long as they are under the control of U.S. trustees. In a recent private letter ruling, the IRS said that an American annuity may be swapped for a foreign annuity that does not engage in business in the United States. The transaction is tax free as long as all the requirements of Section 1035 have been met.

In order to assure compliance with U.S. law when funding retirement plans with foreign products like Swiss annuities, the services of a reputable consultant should be obtained. Asset Strategies International Inc. of Rockville, Maryland is such a company. Two if their representatives, Michael Checkan and Glen Kirsch have special expertise in setting up such accounts in conjunction with Delaware Charter Guarantee and Trust Company, a trust company formed in 1899 and now managing more than $8.5 billion in assets. Asset Strategies International Inc. provides annual year-end currency conversion accounting for clients while Delaware Charter files the reports required by the Internal Revenue Service.

For further information, write the following:
Asset Strategies International, Inc.
1700 Rockville Pike — Suite 400A
Rockville, MD 20852

Chapter Four

British Banking: They Speak Our Language

Americans have many choices when it comes to private banking. Opportunities in the United Kingdom as well as British offshore havens should be considered if for no other reason than the fact that banking in an English-speaking country is quite comforting. Americans and Britons share many customs, but the British are far more likely to keep a private bank account out of the way of prying eyes. An additional benefit for Americans, of course, is that such accounts are immune from U.S. or British withholding taxes. Banks in the United Kingdom will be happy to open and maintain accounts for Americans. Naturally, no social security number need be furnished.

It is important to specify that you are a nonresident when you open such an account. If doing so in person, a passport will suffice as proof. Depositories are divided into two groups. much as they are in the United States. Building societies are the equivalent of American thrifts (like savings and loan associations), organized primarily to promote savings used for home mortgage lending. They usually offer higher yields than the traditional bank counterparts. A few banks which specialize in mail transactions, like the Bank of Scotland, can offer comparably high interest rates. They also offer a full range of investment services in British mutual funds.

As a general rule, British tax inspectors are forbidden from obtaining private account information from their banks. Routine examinations of bank accounts for unusual levels of activity are not authorized by law. By contrast, in the United States all large deposits are automatically reported to the Internal Revenue Service where a roomful of agents keep tabs on American citizens. It is also well know that when British tax examiners learn that an account is owned by a foreigner, the inquiry usually dies at that point despite international agreements between taxing authorities.

In Great Britain, the examination of a private bank account will only occur when a tip from law enforcement authorities on the trail of money laundering or other illegal criminal activity arises. Under a 1989 agreement signed at Basle by many central bank including the Bank of England, deposits which raise suspicion of criminal activities must be reported. British banks have garnered the reputation for harboring large sums of dirty money. By some estimates, as much as three billion dollars in laundered money passes through banks in the United Kingdom and the British Isles each year.

On a more positive note, an account holder is not going to get caught up in an inquiry because the tax authorities randomly targeted his account for examination. The May 1997 landslide win by the Labour Party after eighteen years of Conservative Party rule may have a significant impact on British banking and more specifically British bank secrecy. Only time will tell what changes will occur.

British Banking — Offshore

British offshore bank havens present a someone different picture. Jersey, Guernsey, and Sark are all part of the Channel Islands and are physically located in the English Channel between England and France. For all intents and purposes, these nations are autonomous although their culture is decidedly British. The banks which operate here are by no means uniformly British. In fact, banks like Chase Manhattan and Credit Suisse are among the many which maintain branches in the Channel Islands.

While island residents pay a flat rate on income, nonresidents are not taxed on either interest or dividend payments. Accounts can be held in many different currencies although yields tend to be higher when funds are held as British Sterling. Bank secrecy is not so much embodied in law as it is in custom and tradition here, but account holders can expect exceptional levels of privacy in the Channel Islands. Numbered bank accounts are available for further protection.

The Isle Of Man

In the Isle of Man, a small nation located in the Irish Sea, bank accounts can also be maintained in confidence. Its government has entered into double taxation agreements only with the United Kingdom, making it nearly impossible for other governments or creditors to examine or seize assets held in its institutions. More than fifty banks now operate here, providing a wide range of traditional savings and investment services. Yields are generally very competitive.

Additionally, many annuities are available from local insurance companies. Individual investors can often customize their annuity portfolios, holding the widest imaginable range of securities within these contracts. Such annuities do not have to be reported to the IRS as they are not considered bank accounts. The downside is that such annuities are not generally available to very small investors. Single-premium annuities in which the annuitant makes one up-front payment are often limited to contracts in excess of US $50,000 and may be subject to hefty sales charges. Therefore, these are best suited to investors with substantial assets and long-term objectives.

More will be said about the Isle of Man in a later chapter dealing with trusts and hybrid companies. The Isle of Man hybrid company offers some of the best offshore advantages currently available.

Gibraltar

Gibraltar, located between Spain and Africa, is another offshore tax haven known for banking privacy. The nation has steadfastly resisted pressure from other countries, including the United States, refusing to disclose information on bank accounts maintained within its borders. By some estimates, more than half a million accounts are held here. It is rumored that some of the world's most prominent money launderers do business with banks on Gibraltar. In many ways, this small nation offers the best of several worlds. As a member of the European Union, it enjoys all the advantages of tariff-free international trade. It also boasts near-zero unemployment, the absence of any value added tax (VAT), and some of the lowest corporate tax rates found anywhere in the world. Foreigners who need to maintain privacy in their bank transactions can do so with a high degree of security.

The Cayman Islands

Lastly it is important to mention the Cayman Islands, a group of three small islands located just south of Cuba. As a British crown colony, the Cayman Islands are subject to British rule, but the banking system is completely autonomous. It is hard to believe that a nation of fewer than 40,000 residents plays host to 500 banks and nearly as many insurance companies. More than US $400 billion in funds are currently on deposit in Cayman banks, making it the world's forth-largest financial center.

No direct taxes are imposed on residents or corporations operating in the Cayman Islands. With no income taxes, capital gains taxes, sales taxes, or even inheritance taxes, the government derives what little revenue it needs from import duties, accommodation taxes on tourists, mortgage stamps, and other special duties. For many years, the Cayman Islands were most notable for company and trust services. Today a full array or trust, banking, and world-class investment and brokerage service is available to foreigners.

The Banking and Trust Law of 1966 codified secrecy requirements for banks. Eleven years later, as a result of a U.S. federal court case in which a Caymanian banker was compelled to testify against one of his customers, the Confidential Relationship Law was passed by the legislature. This act imposes strict secrecy responsibilities on banks and other fiduciaries. Officers and employees are severely limited in what information they can access or disclose to others.

Since the 1970's, some erosion in Cayman bank privacy has taken place. The Mutual Legal Assistance Treaty of 1988 signed by both the Cayman Islands and the United States allows for the exchange of information where activities considered criminal under both countries' laws have been alleged. The agreement was primarily constructed to impede the flow of monies obtained from drug deals and other felonious activities. American allegations of tax evasion, provided they do not involve drug trafficking, will *not* trigger the release of proprietary information by Cayman banks, however.

It is important to note that multinational banks operating in the Cayman Islands, especially those headquartered in the United States, may not provide much if any security since they are likely to maintain centralized computer records of all account transactions. If the records are kept in New York or Los Angeles, you might as well kiss off any hope of real banking secrecy. Fortunately, local banks are often able to offer services including credit cards which are processed on-site, avoiding the international information exchange that often accompanies such financial products.

As important as Cayman banks have been in protecting privacy, they are not foolproof repositories. Bowing to American pressures following several recent international scandals, Cayman banks have essentially agreed upon a code requiring them to screen new deposits more carefully. Bankers may now be hesitant to accept suspiciously large deposits from Americans they do not know well. As in all banking situations, it is important for Cayman bank customers to nurture relationships with their bankers to gain long-term trust over time.

Americans returning from the Cayman Islands, particularly those with multiple Cayman entries in their passports, could possibly become targets of Internal Revenue Service audits or investigations. After all, how many times can you tell U.S. Immigration and Naturalization Service inspectors that you have headed south to visit the world-famous turtle farms of Grand Cayman Island? After establishing an account with a Cayman bank, it might be prudent to complete most of your transactions by mail.

For asset management and securities brokerage, Lines Overseas Management Services is one of the most respected businesses operating today. Notable is its independence from onshore influences. It does not have a parent company controlling it from a big country, and does not maintain subsidiaries. Lines Overseas Management clears its trades locally, leaving no paper trail on its client activities in New York, London, or elsewhere.

Rates on certificates of deposit and liquid accounts offered through Lines are generally higher than those available in other markets. The firm offers proprietary Visa Gold debit cards to access cash on deposit. Offshore asset managers are appointed to provide personalized service in the selection of investments in order to best meet specific client needs. These managers fully understand the investment and tax avoidance objectives of overseas customers. Lines is clearly not for everyone, however. It only accepts accounts with US $250,000 minimums. One of its offshore asset managers has been widely recognized in best-selling books and periodicals. He is Scott Oliver, a British subject, who earlier helped to develop sophisticated trading systems for some of Wall Street's largest investment banks. Today, many American estate planning attorneys refer their wealthiest clients to Oliver for financial advice. He has broad familiarity and expertise not only with publicly-traded issues of all kinds, but has a strong track record in private placements.

For more information, contact the following:

> Mr. Scott Oliver
> Offshore Asset Manager
> Lines Overseas Management (Cayman) Ltd.
> P.O. Box 1159GT, Genesis Building
> Grand Cayman, Cayman Islands

Mr. Oliver can be reached by telephone at +1 345 949-5808 or by fax at +1 345 949-1338.

Antigua

Another member of the British Commonwealth of Nations, less known and perhaps less conspicuous to foreign tax authorities is Antigua, also located in the Caribbean Sea. The twin island state of Antigua and Barbuda is primarily known for its pink sand beaches and pristine waters. Antigua attracts half a million visitors each year. Its laws are of course patterned after the British system with an elected parliamentary system. Both major political parties are committed to the continuation of a free-market system with minimum governmental interference or regulation.

With the highest per capita income in the Eastern Caribbean and a government which levies no income taxes, Antigua has attracted some light manufacturing industries. The International Business Corporations Act of 1982 provides fiscal incentives to new corporations.

The Eastern Caribbean Dollar, a multinational currency, is legal tender in Antigua but the U.S. dollar is widely accepted. Antigua has become a center for offshore banking. The largest banks include Barclays, the Royal Bank of Canada, and the Bank of Antigua. The Antiguan government licenses all banks on the island.

Major accounting firms including Coopers and Lybrand, Pannell Kerr Forster, and Price Waterhouse also maintain branches here. Trust and management services are available for larger investors.

Banks in Antigua advertise an exceptional degree of personal and financial privacy, not to mention convenience. Some banks encourage mail and wire transactions for account holders living abroad. Customers can maintain numbered and coded accounts for privacy while earning highly competitive interest rates. The government of Antigua does not levy any taxes on its banks or on income earned by its account holders. There are no withholding taxes, capital gains taxes, inheritance taxes, or costly government reporting requirements. By keeping regulatory bureaucracy to a minimum, banks can pay higher yields on both liquid accounts and certificates of deposit.

Banks in Antigua offer a wide array of services including demand and time deposit accounts denominated in almost any major currency, numbered accounts, letters of credit, foreign exchange, international currency transfers, and portfolio management services. Antigua banks are bound by the provisions of a solid bank secrecy law which forbids bank officers, directors, employees, agents, and auditors from disclosing any account information. Antiguan courts can override this provision but only on compelling evidence that a crime has been committed.

Numbered accounts use randomly selected alphanumeric identifiers. Instructions given by customers for bank wires, payments, or transfers use these numbers only in lieu of names or other conspicuous information. Only the customer and his private banking officer know the true identity of the account holder. A passcode is then added for additional security. It serves as the unique *signature* of the account so to speak.

For those seeking anonymity for business situations, Antigua is one of many places to consider. An Antiguan International Business Corporation can be set up locally at a cost of about US $1,000 including the annual US $250 government fee. Strict confidentiality can be maintained under Antiguan law. Corporations are not required to file any information on their accounts or operations and no public share registers are maintained. Shareholders and beneficial interests need not be disclosed. The corporation can choose to issue bearer shares which are fully transferable.

Also consider that the corporation can conduct business in an environment devoid of income and withholding taxes, stamps, and capital duties. No local directors or shareholders are necessary, there is no minimum capital requirement, capital can be maintained in any currency desired, funds can be transferred worldwide at the direction of the corporation, and annual meetings can be held anywhere in the world. An Antiguan International Business Corporation is particularly suitable for small closely-held businesses since it need only have one director or shareholder. Annual meetings may be held anywhere in the world.

A few words of caution are in order here. Antigua, like a lot of other places around the world, has become a haven for financial fraud. Banks with dubious credentials and motives have sprung up like wild flowers. Those who choose to open accounts in Antigua or elsewhere, particularly if done by correspondence, should make certain they are dealing with reputable institutions. The old adage *caveat emptor,* its English translation *buyer beware,* cannot be overemphasized. Too many people are falling prey to unsubstantiated claims and offers made by unscrupulous offshore businesses which advertise on the Internet and sometimes by direct mail.

Chapter Five

Austria: One of the Last Bastions of Anonymous Banking

Austria is one of several nations where traditional bank secrecy may be short-lived as a direct result of pressure being exerted by its nearby neighbors, the United States, and most significantly sister members of the European Economic Community which it recently joined. As Switzerland began to give in to similar pressures, Austria picked up a fair chunk of its banking business.

The near-collapse of bank secrecy has to some extent been predicated on a domino theory. Nations which bucked in to international pressures to lift bank secrecy soon found their deposits flowing out to others which still respected the individual's right to privacy. Seeing this as an unfair advantages, the weaker nations then pressured their more strong-willed neighbors who in turn gave in as well. Austria is very dependent on its export trade and can't afford to offend its neighbors.

Bank Laws — Following The Swiss

As early as 1979, Austria enacted strict bank secrecy laws which criminalized the dissemination of account information by bank employees and others privy to personal information. Violators were subject to stiff fines and jail sentences. Exceptions to these non-disclosure rules were few and far between. As international pressures began to mount, however, Austria started to rethink its laws. For one, it desperately wanted to be admitted to the European Union. As a direct consequence, its bank secrecy laws were significantly diluted. Money laundering and insider trading became criminal acts, allowing courts to order banks to disclose information on suspected accounts. Tax fraud was added to the list of criminal offenses potentially subjecting bank accounts to audit. Mere tax evasion, however, is still not a crime in Austria. A foreign depositor whose money is not otherwise tainted can safely deposit funds in Austrian banks, knowing that strict bank secrecy will be maintained.

Modest cash transactions, those roughly in excess of US $20,000, must now be reported by banks to Austrian authorities. At one time, reports were only filed when transactions exceeded the approximate equivalent of US $50,000.

Diversity And Economic Stability

In spite of this, there are still some compelling reasons for Americans to consider banking in Austria. The Austrian schilling has historically maintained its strength and by design has been closely linked to the German deutschemark. Austrian nationals pay heavy taxes on bank interest and stock dividends, but foreigners are subjected to much lower rates. To prove that you are not an Austrian resident, you will have to show your passport. Identification details, however, will normally not be taken. If you open an account to trade securities, you will be allowed to do so under a fictitious name or code. You can apply the same identifier to a savings account opened at the same time.

Austrian banks will allow you to transact business in most major currencies. Accounts denominated in Austrian schillings are subject to a government tax of one percent of the distributions made to depositors. As a result, long-term deposits are encouraged. The tax can be avoided, however, by simply maintaining the account in another currency. Certificates of deposit are also except from this charge. Small investors in search of safe savings accounts will find that many banks require so minimums at all.

As a non-resident, you can freely buy securities including Austrian bonds and stocks. As a whole, the Austrian stock market has outperformed most worldwide markets for several years. Securities bought in Austria can be liquidated, the proceeds sent back home or to another country. The securities can also be taken out of the country without further restriction.

The Austrian Sparbuch

One of the most interesting remnants of earlier days of true bank secrecy is the Austrian *Sparbuch*, a truly anonymous savings account which is still alive and well despite a two hundred year history. A *sparbuch* translates in English to a savings book. In appearance it seems like the old-style American passbook savings account, something not very popular anymore in the United States.

Its advantages, however, are immediately obvious. A sparbuch account need not have any name, identification, or address. The issuing bank will not require any references, passport, or other identifying information. The account can be issued to a fictitious name or more commonly to *Ueberbringer* which simply means *passbook holder.* The book's bearer is presumed to be the owner. The account holder can in fact transfer ownership by simply giving the passbook to someone else, along with the *losungswort* or password, an alphanumeric combination selected by the customer when opening the sparbuch account. The bank need not even be informed of the transfer, the sparbuch as negotiable and liquid as cash.

Unlike other types of bank accounts, the sparbuch leaves no paper trail whatsoever. The only records which exist are account numbers and deposit or withdrawal information. Nobody, not even bank employees, know the true owners of these accounts. Deposits can be made in person or by bank transfer. Foreign currencies can be easily converted to Austrian schillings for deposits.

Several disadvantages, however, seriously reduce the value of sparbuch accounts. First, sparbuchs are issued only to Austrian residents. There are several ways to get around this. You might consider establishing Austrian residency, if even for just a few weeks, enjoying the wonderful tastes and sounds of the country. Unfortunately, if you don't speak fluent German you may quickly be recognized as a foreigner trying to get in on a good thing reserved for Austrians.

A number of brokers and law firms in Austria have begun to circumvent these rules by buying sparbuchs themselves, then transferring them to their foreign customers. The bearer accounts are fully transferable so this poses no immediate threat to the new owners. These brokers naturally want to make a few bucks themselves and have been charging notoriously high fees for their services. Acquiring sparbuchs in this fashion is awfully expensive and for most people would defeat the benefits gained. If you happen to have personal business associates or friends residing in Austria, you can have them open your accounts and then transfer them to you, saving you a lot of money.

Two other major disadvantages also make sparbuch investments somewhat dubious. The Austrian government imposes withholding tax on these accounts. The tax is applied to the aggregate sums held by the issuing banks so privacy is not jeopardized. These taxes and other factors nonetheless reduce the interest rates typically paid. With low single-digit yields, sometimes as little as two or three percent, sparbuchs barely keep pace with inflation. The only good reason for using sparbuchs then becomes the ability to squirrel away funds in secrecy. For all intents and purposes, you might as well stash your excess dollars in an overseas safe deposit box.

Chapter Six

Good Things Come in Small Packages: Luxembourg and Liechtenstein

Sadly enough, many Americans could not identify Germany, Switzerland, or Belgium on an unmarked world map. Imagine asking them to find Luxembourg or Liechtenstein, two of the smallest European nations in both land mass and population. Anyone who watches the television show *Jeopardy!* knows that these two names come up repeatedly as correct responses, but you don't have to be a *Jeopardy!* contestant to make money in these nations. For those interested in financial privacy, Luxembourg and Liechtenstein take on even greater meaning.

Luxembourg

Luxembourg has staunchly defended individual rights to bank privacy, fending off pressures from the European Economic Community. Although it is a tiny nation, it plays host to more than 150 banks. Forty percent of the nation's business comes from private banking interests. One of every four Luxembourg residents is employed by the banking community.

Although Luxembourg offers depositors considerable safety, authorities always mindful of banking practices that insure that their institutions remain healthy, the government is less apt to worry whether its customers pay their taxes. This has resulted in large influxes of money from individuals and businesses in Belgium, its neighbor, and from other Common Market countries which impose withholding taxes on their residents. In total, Luxembourg banks now hold more than $150 billion in deposits.

Not surprisingly, the United States has exerted pressure on Luxembourg to cooperate in the investigation of drug and money laundering schemes in which Luxembourg banks have been purportedly used to stash away cash.

So has France and other members of the European Community interested in establishing uniform withholding tax rules and pacts allowing for the free interchange of information among tax authorities. Nonetheless, Luxembourg continued to strengthen its laws guaranteeing bank secrecy.

It is often difficult to insure privacy when regulators are deprived of exposure to a bank's operating practices and portfolios. In Luxembourg, bank secrecy laws are rather lopsided in an effort to both insure privacy and keep banks solvent. Banks are required to disclosed information about their loans in order to insure that their lending practices are prudent. The dissemination of information about deposits, however, is strictly forbidden by law. Prison terms and fines are patterned after Swiss penalties.

One additional safety feature was built into Luxembourg banking law. Not only can't banks disclose information on deposits it holds but its customers cannot waive the provisions of its bank secrecy laws. In other words, a customer who asks his bank to disclose information because he has been threatened by a foreign court will find that his bank ignores his demands. This offers exceptional protection against creditors back home.

Many of Luxembourg's banking customers are corporations and other businesses whose home countries prove unfriendly to their financial needs. In Germany, laws regulating lending ratios force many businesses to look outside national borders for capital. Its decision to impose a 10 percent withholding tax on interest and dividends also caused billions of deutchemarks to flow into Luxembourg banks. Withholding taxes in Switzerland encourage many depositors to seek safe havens for their deposits. In the United States, the imposition of an interest equalization tax drove many American corporations to borrow overseas. Other problems with foreign exchange regulations and reporting requirements among its nearest neighbors also helped Luxembourg banks acquire deposits from abroad..

One-third of Luxembourg bank business is now conducted in U.S. dollars, about 40 percent in German marks. The nation has also seen en exponential growth in the sale of mutual funds, now numbering more than 1000. Because it is a member of the European Union, stamp duties have been eliminated on the purchase and sale of securities originating in other EU jurisdictions.

Small American investors find Luxembourg an attractive banking center for several reasons. Deposits are at least minimally insured by the government up to the rough equivalent of US $15,000. Neither interest nor dividends is subject to withholding taxes and no reports are filed with either Luxembourg or foreign tax authorities on these distributions. For those investing in stocks or bonds, no stamp taxes are payable on their purchase. Gold purchases are also exempt from value added taxes. Luxembourg banks are typically more interested in small deposits than some of their European competitors.

While Luxembourg seemingly offers somewhat better secrecy arrangements than Switzerland, it is more closely tied to other worldwide banking activities than is Switzerland. Any major banking collapse in the United States or Germany is far more apt to affect Luxembourg banks than those in Switzerland.

Potential depositors should also consider the fact that Luxembourg is a signatory to tax treaties with more than a dozen nations including the United States. Because tax fraud is a crime in Luxembourg, it is possible that someone charged with this crime in another country could find his sensitive bank records released by the order of a Luxembourg court.

Liechtenstein

Liechtenstein is another interesting nation, barely 60 square miles in size. Its business interests are someone more diverse than that of Luxembourg with strong manufacturing and service sectors. By the 1980's, several large Liechtenstein-based manufacturers were able to make strong inroads into foreign markets including the United States. Hilti became one of the largest and most prominent manufacturers and marketers of commercial fastening tools for the construction industry. Ivoclar, a dental products manufacturer, became a dominant worldwide manufacturer of artificial dentures.

Although its population is only about 30,000, its per capita income is among the highest in Europe. Liechtenstein can lay claim to only three banks but that is by design. Foreign-owned banks are specifically disallowed by law. Bank in Liechtenstein is under the control of the Prince of Liechtenstein, the head of state, through the intermediary Prince of Liechtenstein Foundation. The government itself owns and controls the second bank, Liechtenstein Landesbank. The third bank is the Vervaltung- und Privatbank, a privately held institution. A fourth bank was chartered a few years ago.

Collectively the three banks are small by international standards but they are important because of their symbiotic relationship with much large Swiss banks. The Liechtenstein banks provide expert investment management services for many holding companies, private foundations, and family foundations some of which maintain accounts in Swiss banks. Proximity to other European nations, the adoption of the Swiss franc as legal tender, favorable tax legislation, and exceptional bank privacy collectively account for the rapid growth of Liechtenstein's banking community. The Banking Act of 1960, already based on a long tradition of secrecy, provided all the security inherent in Swiss law with a few added benefits. With only three banks to supervise, the Liechtenstein government maintains a someone firmer hand in insuring bank privacy.

The state guarantees all deposits without limitation. To the extent that the government has been politically stable all these years and the banks never short on liquidity, the guarantee is probably as good as gold.

Numbered bank accounts are available here, the owners' identities known to just a few bank employees. Personal identification numbers can be used to make transactions. Such accounts are only available to large customers, those with something like $400,000 on deposit.

It is notable that Liechtenstein has not entered into double-taxation treaties with nations other than Austria, and this only to resolve problems created for some of its subjects who work across the border. Likewise, Liechtenstein does not exchange information with tax authorities in other countries. Confidentiality of accounts is insured by both civil and criminal statutes. Banks are required to record the identity of account holders but this information cannot be disclosed to others. Since January 1, 1993, Liechtenstein banks and their employees have been forbidden from revealing any client information acquired in the course of their business dealings. Any such privileged information which might come to the attention of government employees is also protected against disclosure.

Liechtenstein bank law defines the requirements of confidentiality in the widest possible way. It applies not only to information furnished by depositors but also to information banks may acquire from their own research or from third parties. The duties of confidentiality and non-disclosure extend to the families, business partners, and associates of account holders.

Corporate clients can further distance themselves from their banks by appointing an intermediary, usually a Liechtenstein attorney, accountant, fiduciary, or portfolio manager, to

handle transactions. The appointed professional enters into a due diligence declaration in which he declares that he personally knows the identity of the persons who own the deposited assets. He further certifies that to the best of his knowledge the assets were not acquired through criminal conduct. The fiduciary is expected to continue to supervise all future bank transactions with reasonable due diligence and notify the bank of any changes which may occur in the future. In return for this arrangement, the client's true identity is shielded even from the bank.

The Liechtenstein Persons and Companies Law codified the rights of personal and business privacy, opening the door to claims for damages upon breach of confidentiality. This is superimposed on other provisions of the banking law which mandates fines and prison sentences for bankers who violate its non-disclosure provisions.

Banks must comply only with orders of Liechtenstein's own courts. Laws forbid these courts from cooperating with foreign authorities in matters related to political, taxation, or foreign exchange control issues. Banks are specifically prohibited from disclosing the identity of clients and will not routinely share information with governmental authorities. The bank is expected to claim privilege in civil proceedings. Trustees, accountants, and others who work closely with banks are covered under the same provisions of law. The government can demand disclosure only in cases involving domestic criminal prosecutions and in more limited criminal proceedings under the European Convention for Mutual Assistance in Criminal Matters. In the latter case, Liechtenstein courts have the final word as to whether the offense has risen to a level requiring disclosure.

American investors with substantial assets might consider Liechtenstein's banks attractive alternatives to Swiss banks on the basis of stricter security. These banks, however, are primarily interested in acquiring large accounts. For those wishing to avail themselves of discretionary portfolio management services, expect minimums equivalent to US $250,000. Trusts and limited companies are charged a modest annual tax of 0.1 percent of capital, also subject to a minimum, a small price to pay for such privacy.

One totally unique entity available in Liechtenstein is the *anstalt*, translated literally as "the establishment," a design which blends the benefits of a trust with that of a corporation. Its specific characteristics can be tailored to meet individual investment needs. Unfortunately, the IRS as well as several European tax authorities have not been eager to recognize the *anstalt* because of the favorable tax treatment it provides investors.

Other types of family trusts and foundations are available in Liechtenstein too, often providing unusual tax benefits and limited exposure of information to the public. A competent tax attorney familiar with current law should be consulted.

Chapter Seven

Precious Metals

A brief discussion of precious metals is in order here because gold, silver, and platinum can provide special protection against asset erosion, particularly in times of runaway inflation. There are also a couple of good mechanisms for insuring privacy in the purchase and accumulation of precious metals.

A basic rule of thumb suggests that precious metals are best purchased when there is economic pessimism on the horizon. When it appears that major corporations will continue to report upward spiraling profits, investing in equities is a natural choice. The prospect of increased earnings and dividend yields drives stock prices higher. In times of economic boom, real estate has also proven to be an effective tool for wealth accumulation.

Unfortunately, a lot of that has changed. American industrial productivity is low. Labor costs continue to rise. Neither residential nor commercial real estate can offer potential investors much assurance of long-term growth. Indeed, many savings and loan associations were sucked under as a result of massive real estate devaluations and foreclosures in the 1980's. Real Estate Investment Trusts, once thought of as exceptional tools for both the bold and the faint-hearted, proved to be very vulnerable to fluctuations in the economy. Paper assets proved to be very risky in the last twenty years.

For thousands of years, investors have turned towards gold and other precious metals for protection against long-term inflation or other economic uncertainty. Few commodities have this kind of historical performance on which to rely for guidance. The key operative word is *long-term* because precious metals can prove to be quite volatile in the short run.

Tangible assets of this type tend to hold their value for several reasons. First and foremost, they are scarce. Scarcity by definition gives rise to value. Although new finds are not totally uncommon, the world's total resources of gold, silver, and platinum will always be very limited in relation to other minerals. Little more than 120,000 metric tons of pure gold have been mined over six thousand years, about one-third now in the hands of central banks and government agencies worldwide

It is this concept of scarcity that has made gold, and to a lesser extent silver, useful for coinage and moreover as a measure of wealth. Although the United States has essentially abandoned the gold standard, issuing far more paper money than its actual gold reserves, other countries like Switzerland continue to back their currency with gold. Gold has historically maintained its value because of its scarcity, but also because of its symbolism or mystique. When societies over many centuries agree that something has innate value, it retains that value over time.

Second, precious metals do have many useful applications. The higher the demand in relation to supply, the greater their value. Gold, silver, and platinum are all used in jewelry because they are cherished by buyers for their inherent beauty. They also provide the required hardness, durability, and malleability, especially when made into alloys by combining with other metals. Far more important today are their industrial uses. Gold is an exceptional electrical conductor. The most critical electrical connectors are gold-plated. Its resistance to chemicals and abrasion make it ideal for bearings. Its lack of toxicity has led to its use in medical and dental applications.

By late 1997, gold prices had fallen to some of the lowest levels in recent years as the Dow Jones Industrial Average climbed above 8000, providing an excellent opportunity for investors to acquire the precious metal. Remember that gold and other precious metals are best bought as long-term investments and as hedges against major economic downturns. Even the most bullish Wall Street analysts agree that the run-up in stock prices in both the United States and abroad cannot continue indefinitely.

Price-to-earnings ratios, long regarded as the best measures of future stock performance, are preposterously high, suggesting that very significant stock price *corrections* are on the horizon. In effect, investors are not getting value for their dollars when they buy stocks with exorbitant P/E ratios. Some say that the 700 point drop seen in the mini-crash of 1987 was only the tip of the iceberg. A correction of 20 percent or more would not be unreasonable, giving rise to a 1600 point drop in the Dow. Gold prices would probably soar as smart investors take cover and look for tangible assets. What would happen if the stock market *really* crashed, like in 1929? Gold and other precious metals would be among the very few assets likely to keep their value.

Investments in gold therefore make more sense than ever, given the metal's current bargain price and the realistic prospect for a major stock market setback. Even with improvements in mining technology, gold remains a very rare commodity. It has been pointed out that If *all* the gold ever minded were formed into a large cube, it would occupy the space of a modest ten-story office building.

Gold Coins And Bullion

Many investors choose gold in the form of coins for their long-term portfolios. Such bullion coins have been minted by governments or private authorities in the United States, Australia, Great Britain, Canada, Mexico, Austria, and perhaps most notably South Africa. The South African Krugerrand has been regarded by many as the standard for gold coinage. Issued since 1967, each Krugerrand contains exactly one troy ounce of gold. Half- and quarter-ounce gold coins are also minted.

One of the most reliable domestic sources for gold coins is Asset Strategies International, Inc., Suite 400A, 1700 Rockville Pike, Rockville, MD 20852. Their toll-free phone number in the United States and Canada is (800) 831-0007. Because they are not coin dealers in the traditional sense, taking no position themselves in precious metals, they can offer more unbiased service in the purchase and sale of coins through their domestic and foreign networks of wholesalers. More information on the background of the principals, and why I recommend the firm, is at the end of this chapter.

Gold prices will probably continue to show short-term volatility in the years ahead. Unless you have unusually good forecasting skills, you will not always be in a position to make your purchases when worldwide gold prices are low. A sound alternative approach is *cost-averaging,* a technique used for many years by savvy stock and mutual fund investors. Instead of trying to find price bottoms, you arrange to make purchases on a regular periodic basis, perhaps monthly.

If the market price of gold falls, the decrease in your gold portfolio value is offset by the fact that you have bought more at low cost. When prices rise, your high purchase costs are offset by increase in the overall value of your portfolio. Some investors who use cost-averaging make it a point to not even look at the price at which individual purchases have been made. If gold continues to show long-term price appreciation, cost-averaging will provide a sound and systematic way of participating.

Swiss Gold

One of the best programs for gold cost-averaging is known as SwissGold. Customers benefit from the program's ability to buy gold in large quantities on worldwide markets, significantly reducing the costs often associated with small-scale purchases. By buying at wholesale prices and bypassing small order surcharges, clients can save as much as ten percent. Add to that the inherent benefits of cost-averaging which for the average investor can mean additional savings as much as 20 percent. A small investor can quickly accumulate significant holdings of gold as a hedge against long-term inflation or economic downturn.

SwissGold is not only a convenient way to acquire gold but a very safe way. Each customer's holdings is held separately, the bank acting as a fiduciary trust. Gold held by the bank immediately becomes your property, not a mere financial obligation. It can be stored at your option in either Switzerland, the United States, or Canada.

Customers also enjoy the advantages of privacy Swiss bank privacy as detailed earlier. Information on SwissGold programs is available from the following:

> JML Jurg M. Lattmann AG
> Swiss Investment Counsellors
> Baarestrasse 53, Department 212
> CH-6304 Zug, Switzerland.

The firm can be reached by telephone at 41 41 726 5500 or by fax at 41 41 726 5589 (Attention Department 212).

Silver

Like gold, silver is used today in electrical and mechanical applications as well as in jewelry and ornamental pieces. It is a major component in photographic film. Silver also has a long history as a medium of exchange and a storehouse of value. Beginning in 1792, the United States attempted to *fix* the value of silver in relation to gold. The dollar was defined as 24.75 grains of gold or 371.25 grains of silver, making gold precisely 15 times more valuable than silver, ounce for ounce. America was officially on a bimetallic money standard. The English, however, defined the relative value of the two precious metals using a 16:1 ratio. As economies took on a more global character, gold and silver began to vacillate in importance, each one driving the other out of circulation for a time.

The year 1849 marked the beginning of a new era when enormous gold deposits were found and mined in California. Gold slipped in value and silver prices increased. Later that century, silver mines in Nevada and Idaho were discovered, again shifting the balance. The world, even in the late 1800's, was already taking on the qualities of a global economy. Gold and silver prices, especially when set by governments, played havoc on many currencies. By the 1960's, the United States stopped issuing *Silver Certificates*, replacing all paper currency with *Federal Reserve Notes*, backed only by the full faith and credit of the nation. Free market mechanisms were allowed to set the price of gold and silver. Americans were no longer forbidden from acquiring and holding gold in their portfolios.

Silver has shown far more volatility than gold over the long run. It is traded on futures markets in New York, Chicago, and Tokyo. It can also be purchased directly through banks, brokers, and precious metals dealers. Some investors prefer to buy bags of pre-1963 American coins which still had significant silver in them.

Platinum

Platinum also had a history in coinage dating back to eighteenth century Spain, but its primary use was in jewelry manufacture, religious artifacts, and heat-resistant crucibles used in chemical laboratories. Far scarcer than gold, the earth's crust is estimated to contain less than one part of platinum per hundred million parts, most of it mined in South America and in the Ural mountains of Russia.

Although it is still sometimes used in jewelry and there has been a resurgence of interest for investment-grade coinage, platinum is most important today for its unusual chemical problems. It is used as a catalyst to speed up a wide variety of chemical reactions in the manufacture of fuels, plastics, solvents, fertilizers, dyes, textiles, and medicines. It is also widely used in catalytic converters for emission control, not only in vehicles but in heavy industrial applications. As fossil fuels begin to fall out of favor and fuel cell technology explodes, demand for platinum is expected to rise sharply.

Platinum is now traded on major bullion markets worldwide. Futures trading is accomplished at the New York Mercantile Exchange. In Zurich and

London, bullion bars worth about $350,000 apiece are traded regularly. Smaller quantities are routinely traded in Tokyo and Hong Kong. For those interested in investing in platinum coins, the choices are many. Australia, Canada, the Isle of Man, Singapore, Portugal, Russia, and China are among the nations which have issued platinum coins in recent years.

The Mocatta Delivery System

Taking physical possession of large quantities of gold, silver, or platinum naturally involves considerable risk. An excellent alternative is the Mocatta delivery system. The buyer instead of taking physical possession receives a delivery order, a document proving title to his metals. His purchase may be held as serially-numbered gold or silver bars or alternatively as gold, silver, or platinum coins which have been packaged, sealed, and numbered. The owner may choose to store his bullion or coins in either Zurich, Switzerland or Wilmington, Delaware. The depository then countersigns the certificate as proof of its receipt. In either case, the stored bullion or coins are fully insured by Lloyds of London.

The delivery order provided to the buyer is a certificate issued by the Mocatta Metals Group, one of the world's most respected trading groups with offices in New York, London, and Hong Kong. It can be sold, assigned, or used as collateral. The delivery order certificate is itself a non-negotiable instrument, protecting its owner against loss or theft. Because delivery orders are non-negotiable, they may be freely taken in or out of the United States with no reporting required. There is also no IRS reporting requirement on the purchase of such delivery orders..

Mocatta gold may be ordered in one kilobar (32.15 ounce), 100, and 400 ounce sizes. A wide variety of gold, silver, and platinum coins are also available for purchase and storage under the same type of arrangement. Customers pay a modest $100 issuance charge for delivery orders as well as annual storage charges equal to half of one percent of the purchase value, excluding broker commissions. Information on Mocatta orders is available from Asset Strategies International, Inc., Suite A, 1700 Rockville Pike, Rockville, MD 20852. Their toll-free telephone number is (800) 831-0007. They can also be reached by fax by calling (301) 881-1936.

Perth Mint Certificate Program

Another alternative based in Australia is the Perth Mint Certificate Program (PMCP) which allows Americans and others to hold gold and precious metals overseas. It offers the same measures of privacy and security as found in the Mocatta Delivery System. Ownership of metals is established by transferable but non-negotiable certificates. You can take ownership in either specifically allocated coins which are set aside at the Perth Mint in your name or as unallocated shares of the mint's holdings.

Precious metals ownership under the PMCP does not constitute the holding of a foreign bank or financial account under U.S. regulations and therefore entails no American reporting requirements. You nonetheless have the flexibility to transfer your assets at any time to other worldwide financial centers including London, Zurich, or Singapore. The purchase of coins rather than bouillon offers several major advantages. It allows you to take your assets across borders without paying the duties sometimes imposed on bouillon. Coins are available in relatively small denominations and are easily liquidated in major cities worldwide.

Perth Mint Certificate Programs allow you to accumulate gold, silver, platinum, and palladium. Few if any certificate programs offer such diversification, a most useful approach in protecting your assets. When you sell, you can obtain your proceeds in several major currencies including U.S. dollars and Swiss francs. The PMCP's products range in size from 1/20 ounce to 1 kilogram and are considered to be of the highest quality and purity in Australian semi-numismatic coins.

The mint has been in operation since 1899. It is a division of Gold Corporation which is in turn wholly owned and operated by the government of Western Australia. In addition, precious metals holdings are insured at no cost to the buyer by Lloyd's of London. The program thus offers the ultimate in safety and security.

Storage arrangements are handled with the utmost discretion. Clients make transactions using passwords, client numbers, and mint certificate numbers. The mint operates under rules of strict confidentiality and client anonymity, keeping both your holdings and your records offshore and out of public view.

Fees are quite reasonable. Allocated precious metals are subject to storage fees of 1/2% per annum. Unallocated purchases bear no storage fees at all but still maintain excellent liquidity with only one week's notice required for delivery. Each new order is subject to a certificate fee of U.S. $50.00, making it most economical to engage in larger transactions. At the present time, the PMCP minimum opening purchase is U.S. $25,000 with minimum additions of $5,000 allowed at any time. The mint because of its size and reputation is able to purchase metals on worldwide markets at very competitive prices, passing the savings onto individual investors.

Like all precious metals investments, the Perth Mint Certificate Program provides the potential for healthy short- and medium-term growth while offering long-term protection against major economic disasters.

Information on the PMCP can also be obtained from Asset Strategies International, Inc., Suite A, 1700 Rockville Pike, Rockville, MD 20852. Their toll-free telephone number is (800) 831-0007. Their fax number is (301) 881-1936.

Michael Checkan and Glen Kirsch of Asset Strategies International are well known in the financial newsletter industry and at one time or another have been recognized as a "recommended vendor" by many of the writers in the newsletter industry. Among the many writers and publications recommending them are Mark Skousen, Richard Band, Adrian Day, International Living, and Taipan. Adrian Day, editor of Adrian Day's

Investment Analyst says "I've frequently recommended Michael and Glen in the past; you can continue to have confidence in utilizing their services." The principals, Michael Checkan and Glen Kirsch, have been in the foreign exchange business for a combined total of 50 years. They helped the Perth Mint to design this certificate program, using their decades of experience with precious metals and other certificate programs.

Chapter Eight

Offshore Corporations and Trusts

Offshore corporations can be set up worldwide for a variety of purposes including the holding and management of assets, international trading, manufacturing and marketing activities, and tax reduction. Tangible assets like cash and real estate may be held by corporations; intangible assets including patents, copyrights, and trademarks may also be held by corporations. Corporations formed specifically for the purpose of holding intangible assets are especially useful for quickly and economically transferring these assets from owner to owner. Instead of having to sell patent or trademark rights, for example, buyers merely acquire the shares of the existing corporation and all the assets it holds. Active entrepreneurs can establish several separate corporations to help manage different assets or personal needs.

Corporations are treated as legal entities, in a sense *artificial people* in the eyes of the law. Because the corporation is not merely a collection of individuals, but rather a legally-recognized entity on its own merit, it may afford shareholders protection against liabilities arising from its operations. It can sue and be sued, but the individual owners are usually shielded against losses beyond their shareholdings in the corporation. Owners of unincorporated businesses, on the other hand, can lose their own personal assets in the event of successful suits by creditors. Assets including cash, securities, homes, and cars are at risk even if they are totally unrelated to the business conducted by the individual. Under the law, it is impossible to separate the business assets of a sole proprietorship from the personal assets of the business owner. A creditor who goes after a proprietor soon proceeds to seize personal as well as business assets in satisfaction of any judgments.

While domestic corporations provide protection for individual shareholders against such *personal* seizures, they still leave shareholders open to litigation against the corporation itself. Corporate assets including cash holdings, bank deposits, office equipment, and accounts receivable are still at risk. The foreign corporation offers significantly more protection because assets can be kept out of public view. Its owners can often remain completely anonymous and judgments obtained in one country may be difficult if not impossible to enforce in another country where the business is incorporated.

Foreign corporations may also convey benefits analogous to foreign citizenship, providing trade advantages not available to outsiders. By establishing a corporation in a particular jurisdiction, entrepreneurs can often exact reduced trade tariffs and barriers.

People sometimes talk about corporate *shells* which can either be established from scratch or purchased. The term *shell* merely implies that a corporate structure exists with no current activity taking place. The shell, a corporation chartered by the local jurisdiction, however, is every bit as legal as a major multinational corporation doing billions of dollars of business. It can be formed by local incorporators, have as few as one owner and director, and can exist with virtually no assets. It need not have an office or staff. It can operate out of the desk drawer of its appointed service agent. In order to simplify and speed up the process of incorporating, some people choose to buy already-chartered corporate shells which were set up specifically for the purpose of being sold and operated by new owners.

For many, the offshore corporation's primary benefit is privacy or anonymity. The corporation's name need not have any relationship to your own name; indeed, you can usually select any name you wish for your corporation as long as it has not already been taken by another incorporated entity within the same jurisdiction. An offshore corporation allows an investor or entrepreneur to conduct business activities in a manner which makes it difficult for potential creditors or poachers to cause financial damage.

The choice of offshore corporate locations should be predicated on several factors. Cost is naturally one of them. Generally speaking, offshore corporations can be quickly chartered with the help of local counsel for less than $3000. In some instances, costs can be as low as $575. All jurisdictions require that a local agent be named solely for the service of process; the agent receives an annual fee. The government which issues the corporate charter will also charge an annual franchise fee or tax. Together, these maintenance fees might cost the corporation another $500 to $1000 annually.

Before setting up a foreign corporation, you should also consider the relative political stabilities of the competing choices. A nation which is stable and neutral is likely to provide a better environment for international trading than one which is earmarked by many enemies. It is also important to find a jurisdiction whose courts are friendly to its corporations in the event of lawsuits. Perhaps most importantly, corporate domiciles which guarantee confidentiality and at the same time minimize reporting requirements should be favored. The establishment of an offshore corporation should not bring with it a torrent of filing and regulatory requirements.

In setting up an offshore corporation, it is important to consult with an advisor who understands the benefits, limitations, and intricacies inherent in such ventures.

One consulting business specializing in the formation of offshore corporations and trusts is Britannia Corporate Management Limited, located in the Cayman Islands. Its president, Gary F. Oakley, is a Canadian with 17 years of Cayman Islands residency. Britannia is licensed to manage investment holding and trading companies, real estate holding companies, patent holding companies, and insurance holding companies. It is licensed to incorporate and manage corporations registered in the Cayman Islands. As such, the firm can service as the registered office of a corporation, provide its secretary, officers and directors, or undertake any day-to-day functions that may be required. More information can be obtained by writing the following:

Britannia Corporate Management Limited
Attn: New Clients Information
P. O. Box 1968
Whitewall Estates, Grand Cayman
Cayman Islands

Britannia can be reached by fax at +1 345 949 0716, directing your communication to New Clients Information.

Foreign Corporate Bank Accounts

If your corporation intends to do business internationally, it will undoubtedly want to maintain an account with a strong and reputable foreign bank. Even the largest multinational banks which maintain offices in foreign jurisdictions are bound by local laws and customs. The clear advantage of banking with larger institutions is protection against bank failure because they are well capitalized and their risks are spread widely. When dealing with smaller banks, local investor protection programs may be inadequate for your corporation's needs. Insurance is often afforded only for modest deposits and then sometimes only in local currencies.

Also consider that greater privacy is sometimes achieved in dealing with smaller but well capitalized banks whose records are maintained locally. An added bonus of dealing with smaller local banks is that they are often more autonomous, allowing them to make loans, accept letters of credit, and make other financial decisions quickly and with less bureaucratic red tape.

It is also important to question a bank's international finance experience — its ability to routinely process letters of credit and deal with multi-currency and cross-border issues. Make certain that the bank you select can handle instructions by fax or phone if that is what you require; many offshore banks will not honor such requests. Finally, you will undoubtedly want to work with a bank whose employees are fluent in your native language.

Corporations can change the names of signatories, the people it authorizes to make deposits and withdrawals, at any time. This is done by a simple corporate resolution, signed by the directors, and presented to the chosen bank. Computerized records at such banks tend to reflect corporate account names rather than personal signatories, adding another layer of confidentiality should prying eyes gain access to bank records. Anyone on a hunting expedition trying to find you will not routinely come across your name in the course of a search. Bear in mind that most foreign laws also provide stronger protection against the arbitrary release of bank records anyway, so disclosure is highly unlikely in any event.

Offshore Trusts

While corporations have to be owned by other entities, either individuals or other corporations, trusts in effect own themselves. The distinction is important when you consider the tax consequences of corporations and trusts. Corporate shareholders are generally responsible for paying income taxes on distributions made to them by their corporations as dividends. Both profits from operations and capital gains are taxable during the course of a corporation's life or upon its liquidation. The corporation may itself pay corporate taxes on all of its profits, before dividends are distributed to shareholders, giving rise to the expression *double taxation*.

The trust, like the corporation, is considered a separate legal entity. The trust is a legal device which allows title and possession of property to be held by one person, the *trustee*, for the benefit of one or more other persons, the *beneficiaries*. A trust can hold title to virtually any type of assets. It can conduct business much like a corporation. It can be used to dole out money to the elderly or pay medical or educational bills. One of the major benefits of the trust is that it can streamline inheritance processes, avoiding the costly and time-consuming hurdles of probate.

Unlike the corporation, however, the trust has no outside owners to whom taxing authorities can look for money. A *grantor* creates and funds the trust, determining the rules by which the trust will operate, legally called the *declaration*. The powers granted to the trustee may be very broad or much more narrowly defined. They control the way the trustee manages the trust's assets during the grantor's life and after his death. One or more *beneficiaries* are named by the grantor; they will receive distributions as provided in the trust's guidelines. The day-to-day operations of the trust are placed in the hands of a *trustee* who decided, within the guidelines originally established, how assets are to be prudently invested and distributed. Banks, trust companies, and other specially-trained financial advisors are often appointed as trustees.

Although a single individual can theoretically take on all three roles — grantor, beneficiary, and trustee — such a trust will normally provide little or no asset protection or tax relief. This is also true of domestic revocable trusts in which the grantor reserves the right to terminate the trust at any time and regain the assets.

Offshore trusts can provide significant measures of both asset protection and privacy. The names of grantors and beneficiaries need not be a matter of public record. Nonetheless, if you appoint yourself as beneficiary of the offshore trust, tax authorities at home may take the position that because you continue to benefit from the trust, its assets should remain at risk in the event a creditor goes after them. You can limit this liability by establishing a trust in which you are given a beneficial interest only in the income generated by the trust but not the initial capital placed in the trust. A much safer approach is to remain at arm's length from your trust, naming family members as beneficiaries..

For the same reason, it is best to appoint an independent trustee to manage the trust's day-to-day operations. In determining whether a trust has a legitimate purpose, something other than mere tax avoidance, a court at home is likely to consider the degree to which you have distanced yourself from the trust. Offshore trustees are of course not bound by rulings of courts or administrative bodies in your home country, providing further protection against creditors, forfeitures, and seizures. The trustee should be selected carefully, knowing that you are placing in his hands the control of your valuable assets.

In some foreign countries, the grantor may also name a *protector* for the trust, an individual who overseas the trustee. A protector has the power to fire and replace the trustee if he believes the trust is not being managed in accordance with the rules originally set out. The grantor can serve as protector, but in the event of a dispute in a home court such an arrangement might again raise red flags about the degree to which the trust has been operated independently of those with a beneficial interest.

Offshore trusts are frequently used for international investment purposes. Although the foreign trustee makes actual investments of assets within the trust, you can certainly participate by phone or letter in suggesting particular strategies or investment vehicles. Privacy and confidentiality are assured, domestic reporting requirements are drastically reduced, taxes are avoided, diversification is achieved, and financial flexibility is greatly enhanced.

Switzerland is often selected as a venue for the creation of trusts for all the reasons outlined in an earlier chapter. Swiss law provides investors with most of the tools necessary to assure secrecy, promote capital preservation, protect against creditors, and reduce tax liabilities. Moreover, the creation of trusts in Switzerland is backed by long legal tradition.

In creating a trust, it is exceedingly important to select a country and an advisor wisely. Bogus trusts that purport to take title and possession of assets but which have clearly been set up solely for the purpose of defrauding creditors often prove worthless. In many instances, physical assets remain in the home country, perhaps in banks or brokerage houses. In the United States, federal and state courts frequently declare such trusts to be shams and accordingly order the seizure of such assets to pay creditors. The maintenance of a *paper trust*, often created at significant cost by a trust mill, offers no real protection.

A discussion of legitimate offshore trusts would not be complete without also mentioning the small West Indies island nation of Nevis. Located about 225 miles east of Puerto Rico, Nevis is part of the St. Kitts-Nevis nation, a former British colony. Although the two-island nation is tiny with a resident population estimated at 10,000, it is of great interest in financial circles. St. Kitts-Nevis maintains membership in the United Nations, the Organization of American States, and the Caribbean Community. As an associated Commonwealth participating state in the European Union, it offers significant trading benefits to local businesses.

The Nevis government, which incidentally maintains a constitutional right to secede from the slightly larger St. Kitts, imposes no taxes on its residents. It encourages the formation of local corporations and trusts and provides many benefits to foreign investors. Its 1994 International Trust Ordinance was specifically designed to provide foreigners the ultimate in asset protection. When an asset protection trust is established in Nevis, assets are fully protected against foreign creditors, plaintiffs of all kind, and foreign governments. Nevis has been found useful as a shield by physicians and doctors concerned with outrageous malpractice judgments as well as corporate officers and directors faced with judicially-imposed liability arising in the course of their business dealings.

When a Nevis-based asset protection trust is properly formed and maintained, the nation's courts will not honor judgments rendered by courts in other jurisdictions, forcing creditors and other plaintiffs to refile their cases in Nevis courts. Complainants must post $25,000 bonds to cover court costs before litigation can proceed. Additionally, under the statute of limitations covering asset protection trusts, plaintiffs have only one year following the formation of such trusts to bring suit. Where plaintiffs allege fraud by the trust, its officers, or beneficiaries, the burden of proof is squarely placed on the shoulders of the claimant.

Asset protection trusts in Nevis also convey privacy rights. Trust documents need not be filed with any government agency and information is kept out of all public records. The trust is easily formed, paperwork limited to the naming of a trustee, dates of trust formation and filing, and the appointment of a local trust company. The trust pays a $200 filing fee and an additional $200 annual maintenance fee. One person may serve as the trust's grantor or *settlor*, beneficiary, and protector.

The trust's creator names the trustees empowered by the declaration to manage the assets that have been transferred to the trust. In most cases, three trustees are appointed, only one of whom needs to be in Nevis. The local trustee serves as the protector; although he plays no role in the day-to-day management of trust assets, the protector assures compliance with the trust's objectives as well as local law.

The Hybrid Company

An interesting alternative to the trust is something called the *hybrid company*, an alternative structure available today in the Isle of Man. This type of arrangement evolved because English law never provided for the formation of non-profit corporations. Instead, ordinary companies were formed with members agreeing to guarantee the debts incurred by their organizations in small finite amounts. In reality, this analogous to the manner in which U.S. corporate shareholders guarantee the debts of their corporations to the extent of their individual stock investments.

The hybrid company came into being by combining a guarantee company with a more traditional share-issuing company under a single umbrella. Today, hybrid companies serve the needs of wealthy investors in situations where regular trusts are too restrictive or are unavailable for a variety of reasons. Hybrid companies can operate as quasi-trusts or what has been called *incorporated trusts*, providing the same benefits as conventional trusts under a someone more complex organizational design.

People living in civil law jurisdictions where the typical Anglo-Saxon Trust is not understood or recognized by their governments can make good use of the Corporate Trust structure created by the hybrid company. Civil code countries may recognize trusts created outside their borders, but not when created by their own residents. The same rule of thumb applies to common law countries; they will recognize trusts only to the extent that they are created by individuals whose own domiciles recognize such trusts.

In still other countries, individuals may not normally be given the option of choosing their heirs, their governments instead determining who inherits the estates of decedents. In these situations, hybrid company trusts ensure that estates are disposed of according to the wishes of their owners.

Corporations are rather universally recognized and accepted, even in those jurisdictions which do not recognize trusts. The hybrid company, a vehicle with a corporate structure, thus provides a recognized means of separating the legal ownership of assets from those with a beneficial interest in them. A shareholding member of the hybrid company can retain control of assets but may not benefit from them. In this capacity, he can protect the assets against the future threats of creditors. Guarantee members, on the other hand, are analogous to beneficiaries of a trust. They are legally considered guarantors, not shareholders, and are thus not required to disclose their interest in the trust, providing significant anonymity.

When a guarantee member dies, his membership ends much as a partner's membership ends in a partnership upon his death. Membership does not pass to family or heirs on death nor can it be transferred during his lifetime. New guarantee members can instead be elected to fill the void.

The relationship between shareholding member and guarantee member enables the hybrid company to function as a trust. A shareholding member would normally have the right to income and assets upon the termination of a company, generally in proportion to the capital contributed to the company during its life. A guarantee member does not normally contribute capital; he only pays in an agreed-upon amount necessary to guarantee debts of the company. He may or may not have rights upon liquidation, depending on the terms of the Articles of Association, the governing rules of the hybrid company.

When used for trust purposes, the hybrid company's management is placed in the hands of shareholding members and directors. They are prohibited from receiving any financial distributions. Guarantee members on the other hand receive dividends and can avail themselves of other benefits such as low-interest loans. They do not actively participate in the company's decision-making process and generally do not vote in elections. In effect they become beneficiaries of the trust that has been created.

Individuals as well as charitable organizations and family foundations can benefit immensely from the asset protection, privacy, and tax advantages of the hybrid company. Arrangements are very complex, however, and should only be undertaken by an advisor fully skilled in this structure. Americans are especially cautioned to make certain that the requirements of the Internal Revenue Service are met to avoid later difficulties.

The foremost expert in hybrid companies is Skye Fiduciary Services Limited. Under the direction of its chairman, Charles Cain, formerly managing director of the second merchant bank to open in the Isle of Man, Skye Fiduciary is the most experienced offshore corporate and trust management business in the jurisdiction. Although Skye offers a full range of company and trust management services, their expertise in designing novel company structures to meet the needs of foreign clients is unique.

For further information, write the following:
> Skye Fiduciary Services Limited
> Attn: New Clients Department
> 2 Water Street
> Ramsey, Isle of Man 1M8 1JP
> United Kingdom

Their telephone number is +44 1624 816117. Fax service is available at +44 1624 816645; direct communications to New Clients Information.

Chapter Nine

Offshore Privacy: Issues Beyond Banking

The chairman of an up-an-coming publicly-traded American corporation was recently diagnosed with prostate cancer. Fortunately his malignancy was of a type and at a stage with an excellent prognosis for full recovery. Knowing how sensitive stockholders are to the health of their leaders on whom they depend for management guidance, the CEO carefully arranged to take a couple of weeks of vacation. He quietly checked into a hospital a few hundred miles from his company's executive offices for the required treatment, hoping to keep himself out of the limelight.

These precautions proved to be inadequate. Within days of his hospital admission, word of his illness leaked throughout the business and investment communities. His company's stock plummeted almost 20 percent, reducing the corporation's equity by millions of dollars. Some individual shareholders, including the chairman himself, lost tens and in some cases hundreds of thousands of dollars. Rumors, whether founded or not, can be economically devastating for individuals as well as their businesses.

Medical Records Privacy

There are many reasons to shield your medical records from public scrutiny. The mere fact that you have had an illness, even when it has been completely controlled or cured, can cost you and your family millions of dollars. Despite the supposed protections of law, health problems routinely result in the denial or loss of employment, the cancellation or loss of insurance benefits, and serious economic losses such as those suffered by the CEO we just discussed.

A business executive with an illness perceived to be life-threatening becomes a pariah in the eyes of his colleagues. A sports figure with a potentially disabling illness or injury finds himself put out to pasture. An actress with drug or alcohol problems falls out of the good graces of casting executives and producers. A law enforcement officer or fire fighter who develops mildly-elevated blood pressure finds himself out of work even though the condition is completely controllable with medication.

Despite canons of ethics which require that physicians, hospitals, and other health care providers maintain patient records in strict confidence, information leaks in the United States are rampant. It is easy to find out whether someone you know has been hospitalized. Just call the hospital's desk and ask for the room number of someone you suspect is a patient. In seconds, your suspicions will be confirmed. Hone in on an innocent breakfast conversation among nurses who have just left their facility; you are likely to hear shop talk about difficult patients they have cared for during the night.

If you followed the Menendez brothers trial in California, you know that a psychiatrist who provided therapy for the pair testified about their alleged confession at their criminal trial; so did the physician's girlfriend who admitted spying on the doctor and his clients. What was once believed to be privileged medical information isn't so privileged anymore. Sometimes information leaks from health care facilities are far more benign but nonetheless potentially damaging. When an envelope stuffing machine recently went haywire in Florida, one customer of a large clinical laboratory received the itemized bills of several dozen other clients whose patient numbers happened to follow his own. The paperwork included diagnosis codes, lists of tests run by the laboratory, even the names of all the referring physicians and their insurance companies.

Then there is the problem of medical reporting. The Medical Information Bureau as well as other repositories of information maintain computerized files on millions of Americans with no guarantee that the information is even vaguely correct. Like credit reporting agencies, these bureaus collect millions of pieces of data annually and then redistribute the information to insurers, employers, and others keen on invading your privacy.

Suppose you go to your physician for a routine physical examination. A nurse attempts to draw blood for routine analysis but has difficultly obtaining an adequate sample so she repeatedly sticks your arm to collect a greater volume of blood. There is now a good probability that the serum will have become hemolyzed as a result of its rough handling. The next thing you know is that the results come back showing very abnormal liver function tests. Although the physician is likely to re-run the tests, there is a good chance that somewhere in cyberspace there will be a report showing abnormal liver functions. Perhaps you may even be labeled a chronic alcoholic by someone who receives and misinterprets the erroneous information.

More and more American executives, public figures, and others vulnerable to damage from medical information leaks are now taking their medical treatment needs offshore. Exceptional medical facilities are available throughout Western Europe and Japan for major surgical procedures, cancer and AIDS treatment, cardiac care, and other serious conditions. Treatments for more routine ailments like hypertension, diabetes, back pain, drug addiction, and impotence are available in an even wider array of places. Making the decision to seek medical treatment overseas in order to maintain your privacy does not necessarily mean sacrificing the best available care. On the contrary, physicians in Europe and Japan are not constrained by agencies the U.S. Food and Drug Administration in offering the latest treatments and pharmaceutical products. The FDA has been notorious for dragging its feet, sometimes for decades, in approving new medical procedures and medications even in the face of epidemics.

You must be prepared to sacrifice insurance reimbursement if you choose to take your medical problems offshore. Some variation of universal or nationalized health care is available to legal residents of virtually every nation throughout the industrialized world, the United States being the singular exception. Naturally you will not be eligible for this kind of free or deeply subsided care if the sole purpose of your visit is to get medical attention. Many private physicians and hospitals, however, will accommodate you on a pay-for-service basis. Fees in Western Europe for foreigners seeking treatment are typically 40 to 60 percent lower than in the United States for comparable services so the financial burden will be lessened. Most important, there will be no sharing of social security numbers, diagnoses, or medical records with others. You will be able to return home, knowing that your health records will not be disseminated to those who have no right to see them.

Safe Deposit Boxes

If you do business offshore, you should also consider the vulnerability of safe deposit boxes you maintain for the storage of negotiable certificates, foreign currency, precious metals or certificates evidencing its your ownership of bullion, or financial records. A secure box may prevent losses from fire or common theft, but it may also open a can of worms in the event of your death or incapacity.

In general, American safe deposit boxes are sealed upon the death of their box holders. The bank may be forbidden by law from denying access to your spouse or beneficiaries until your executor makes appropriate arrangements. The federal government as well as your state government will hover like vultures over your box, hoping to find assets that they can tap for their own coffers. The IRS may even send an agent to observe the opening of your box. If your box contains assets that you were holding in trust for your children, there is a good probability that Uncle Sam will treat these assets as having been yours, subjecting them to estate taxes. Should IRS agents find evidence of offshore accounts that had not been reported, the government might attempt to seize them.

It is therefore essential that you make arrangements to store your valuables, particularly those relating to offshore accounts or business, in a more secure fashion — one that will permit those you desire to gain access to your valuables upon your death. A relatively simple solution can be found by forming a corporation whose sole purpose is to maintain a safe deposit box. This is a perfectly legal technique which can be done literally in a matter of minutes, no attorney required. Several states including Delaware and Nevada are particularly friendly to corporations. Several services can do this for you by phone or Internet for about one hundred dollars. Maintaining a corporation requires minimal effort including holding an annual meeting of the directors. Of course, the legitimate corporation can have as few as one director, so this poses no problem as long as you declare and hold a meeting once each year.

Corporations which do business in other states are termed *foreign corporations* and are normally required to pay a small annual franchise fee to those states in which it conducts businesses. Holding a safe deposit box is not considered the conduct of business, eliminating this additional nuisance. Since the corporation is an artificial person under the law, the death of any of its shareholders will not affect the corporation's access to its safe deposit box. The corporation's board of directors merely authorizes certain people to have access to the box and provides a copy of the resolution to the bank. The corporation can of course change the names of those authorized to open the box by issuing new resolutions at any time. In effect, the corporation isolates you as an individual from the corporation which you wholly own.

Chapter Ten

The Cashless Society

For thousands of years, civilizations effectively allocated and stored wealth by adopting currency systems. The key characteristics of any such system included scarcity, resistance to counterfeiting, the ability to make change, durability, and portability.

Gold and silver proved more useful than most elements because they were scarce and thus intrinsically valuable. On the other hand, although water could well have been used in a desert society plagued by perpetual drought, its adoption as currency in the rain forests of South America would not have worked.

There have certainly been attempts to counterfeit legal tender in every society. Metallurgists quickly learned how to produce alloys that *looked* like gold and the experts quickly responded with analytical tests to determine what was real and what wasn't. Paper currency was soon substituted for the real thing. Its advent of course created many opportunities for skilled technicians with printing presses. Uncle Sam began inserting special red and blue threads in American bills. It also formulated special inks containing ferromagnetic materials and adopted laws making it illegal to produce or be in possession of special papers used exclusively for currency production. In spite of all this, the Treasury Department still has its hands full with counterfeiting operations, many of then conducted outside the United States. Next generation currencies will contain holograms and other special features as governments try to fight back.

Central banks used to prefer currencies which were reasonably durable so that bills would not have to be replaced frequently as they physically wore out. In the United States, however, the Bureau of Engraving and Printing moved in the opposite direction. It began using water-based inks in its printing operations, inks which held up poorly under the demands of normal use. Some say that this was intentional. The creation of currencies with very short lives helps regulators track money flows.

Does Anyone Remember Cash?

Cash transactions soon gave way to asset exchanges by checks and other negotiable instruments. Western governments found the trend especially exciting. They soon realized that an economic system flooded with checks literally *created money*. When an individual deposited $1000 in his checking account and immediately wrote a check for $1000 to another person, the money supply doubled during the period of float, the time it took for the check to clear. Of course the recipient of that check might have done the same thing at his own bank, effectively tripling the money supply in circulation. This is what economists called the *multiplier effect*. What a convenient way to expand the money supply without mining a single ounce of gold!

In any case, the expansion of money became so complicated and so potentially threatening to the collapse of national economies that governments were forced to create monstrous agencies like the Federal Reserve System to regulate money supplies. Today we hear of M-1, M-2. and M-3, successively broader measures of the money in circulation in the United States.

Checks — Convenient But Easily Traceable

A second and perhaps more onerous reason for celebrating the check was the fact that it was largely more trackable than good old fashioned cash. The Federal Reserve System was also charged with the operation of clearing houses, agencies which process the millions of checks presented daily for payment in the United States. Today it is a highly automated process which assures that checks clear their respective banks quickly, usually within a day or two. The money trail left behind, however, is indelible.

Everything is microfilmed and everything is ultimately available to federal, state, and local investigators.

Creative folks of course found work-arounds even in the face of regulations that were aimed at destroying what little privacy we still had left. An individual or business, for example, could simply deposit checks that were received in overseas banks. A little more security could be added by selectively endorsing the received check to a third party who would then deposit it offshore. There would of course be a clear paper trail for the check writer, but unless government snoops had some reason to link the payer with the check's recipient, the check might well go unnoticed.

Credit Cards — The Collapse Of Privacy

The explosion in credit card issuance further delighted the government. Money supplies could again be expanded, further diluting the real value of the dollar. As for information gathering, credit cards were nearly perfect. Every transaction left a computer entry. Large merchants moved quickly to point-of-purchase transactions, leaving paper trails in real time. Government agents could not only track how much an individual spent but where and on what products or services. A person who spent more than he purportedly earned could be assumed to have under-reported income or engaged in criminal activity. With the exception of transactions made with credit cards that had been issued and cleared by offshore banks, VISA and MasterCard gave government officials exactly the surveillance tools they wanted.

Money Laundering

Anyone who thought that money laundering was not serious business learned the hard way. A federal judge in Providence, Rhode Island handed down a 600-year prison term in 1993 to a man convicted of money laundering. His own bankers had brought suspicious activities to the attention of federal agents. Under the Annunzio-Wylie Money Laundering Act of 1992, financial institutions, their directors, officers, employees, and agents were specifically granted immunity from civil liability for filing such reports. Moreover they were held harmless for failure to notify their customers that such reports had been filed. Your bankers, the people you had thought you were paying to protect your assets, had become unpaid informants of the federal government.

American Express suffered a $7 million fine and an additional $7 million forfeiture for failing to detect what the government believed were cases of money laundering. As part of the agreement to settle the matter for a small fraction of what Uncle Sam initially demanded, the company also signed a consent order requiring it to spend another $3 million in employee training so that it could better spy on its account holders.

The term *money laundering* has taken on such broad connotations and a life of its own that for all intents and purposes it means little more than transferring assets without telling Big Brother. When U.S. attorneys find that they are unable to prove the existence of any *actual* crime like grand larceny, drug dealing, or child pornography, they charge defendants with money laundering, a crime that sticks like glue in federal courts. Such convictions often carry heavy fines and forfeitures, making such courts looks more like cash registers than judicial bodies searching for the truth.

As governments began intruding further and further into the private financial lives of its people under the guise of law enforcement when its intent was really tax collection, smart folks started reacting with measures of their own. The 1980's saw the return of simple barter arrangements, something that had not been popular in the United States for more than a hundred years. Joe the Barber contracted with Ernie Cool Wrench, trading haircuts for oil changes. Although these were reportable as income under IRS rules, barber police had not yet been deputized. In some instances, multi-million dollar barter transactions have now replaced traditional cash-for-service deals. Many of these are now conducted by Americans overseas. A well-respected American real estate broker, for example, waived his customary commission on the sale of an expensive condominium to a European dentist who in turn provided him with dental implants.

Smart Cards — Convenience And Anonymity

The latest entry into the fracas between governments and their subjects surrounds a relatively new technology, the *smart card*. Unlike conventional credit cards whose magnetic stripes contain limited information such as credit card numbers and personal identification numbers, smart cards contain embedded microchips with the capacity to hold far more information. Depending on how they are used, or more precisely how they are regulated by governments, they can prove to be blessings in privacy or the worst nightmares yet to come.

Smart cards, unlike credit cards, can act like self-contained refillable storage chests of money. The cards can be taken to banks or special vending machines where they can be refilled. When a merchant accepts a smart card for a purchase, he obtains a code which he then takes to his friendly banker or bank card company and trades it for cash. The cash value of the smart card is automatically reduced by the same amount at the time of purchase. Like true cash, the cards are portable, highly tamper-proof, and resistant to forgery. Stored value cards, like cash, can also offer the ultimate in privacy. All information stored on these cards is strongly encrypted, assuring that only authorized users gain access.

It is important to understand the distinctions among the variety of smart cards currently available. Both MasterCard and Visa have been issuing disposable cards as well as stand-alone reloadable cards in Europe and more recently in the United States. The disposable cards operate much like prepaid telephone calling cards. They are bought over-the-counter, are not linked to their customers by social security number, name, bank account, or any other identifier, and are simply discarded once the cash value has been depleted. The cash equivalent is literally embedded in the card, leaving no paper or computer trail.

American investors who do a lot of business overseas might benefit by using prepaid calling cards for the same reasons of privacy. The calls of course would have to be made from pay telephones not otherwise linked to the card holders. Naturally all calls made from home or the office, even though charged to anonymous phone credit cards, leave paper trails.

Reloadable smart cards are also becoming more readily available from major vendors worldwide. These can be recharged with cash whenever residual balances get low. Some newer phone cards operate this way as well. They can be left out on a self-service counter because they are devoid of value until activated by the cashier at time of purchase.

The Japanese have made heavy use of laser optical cards which fall somewhere between true chip cards on conventional magnetic stripe cards. Each can hold about four megabytes of data, written and read with a laser beam, enough to store a significant amount of information.

Smart cards which are linked to existing credit or debit cards provide little benefit beyond convenience. Privacy is of course compromised and by preloading cash at the front end the consumer loses the interest-free grace period he would otherwise have enjoyed with a conventional credit card.

Another major use of smart cards of either the optical or chip variety, is in medical information storage. An individual can store all kinds of vital information on medical problems, drugs taken, even digitized cardiograms, all with the same encrypted security available to smart bank cards. Authorization to read these cards can be selectively given to physicians or others who need to know, keeping confidential information out of the hands of other predators.

By some estimates, over one billion smart cards are issued annually, the vast majority prepaid telephone cards. Fewer than ten percent are general purpose cards issued by financial institutions. International standards are now being written to assure that chip cards issued in one nation will be fully usable in another as is now the case with magnetic stripe cards.

Some observers say that smart cards will ultimately outsmart governments bent on destroying what little privacy still exists. They believe that financial transactions, telephone calls, and medical records can one day be handled again with personal security against prying eyes. Smart cards can assure customers complete anonymity but this requires both the card issuer and the customer to take certain precautions. The card should not carry a name or signature. It should be self-standing, i.e. not linked to any bank account or traditional credit card account. Customers should avoid the use of such cards in retail situations where they may also be asked to furnish names and addresses, for example in connection with product warranty registrations or mail-in rebates.

In the United Kingdom, trials of a smart card marketed under the Mondex brand proved very successful. Mondex, a joint venture of British Telecom, Midland Bank, and National Westminster Bank is a multiple-purpose card capable of cash storage, foreign currency exchange, telephone bank functions, and telephone charge applications. Cards can be reloaded by Mondex phone at any time. Those who opt for a Mondex wallet, a small hand-held card-reading device, can also transfer money directly from card to card without ever accessing any bank or card issuer's computer. Once money is withdrawn from a bank and loaded into one of these cards, purchases can be made with complete anonymity. The Bank of England, the United Kingdom's central bank, is under pressure from the intelligence community to develop policies which would create paper trails.

Many privacy experts aren't so sure that smart cards will ultimately improve individual security against intrusions. Governments are looking for ways to integrate smart card technology into national identity cards. Americans have so far resisted the idea of national identity cards, but the idea keeps surfacing in Washington and may soon become reality. The most common reasons cited include the need to better control immigration and prevent fraud in the disbursement of government funds. President Clinton proudly waved a prototype card before audiences when he was touting universal health coverage.

Such cards have been in use for many years in places like Germany, Italy, Singapore, Korea, and Brazil. They usually contain information including the holder's name, date and place of birth, registration number, and in some cases permanent or temporary addresses. Malaysian identity cards also contain information on religion, ethnicity, and physical characteristics. Photographs and fingerprints are not at all uncommon on national identity cards.

The application of new technologies to national identity cards could soon enable governments to encode anything it wants — arrest and driving records, personal financial information, medical and insurance histories, domestic and foreign travel itineraries that have been undertaken, and much more.

Chapter Eleven

Drastic and Not-So-Drastic Measures

With privacy issues seemingly on everyone's mind and unwarranted intrusions becoming more malignant every day, it is not surprising that many individuals would resort to drastic measures to protect their assets and even their identities. It is important, however, to carefully examine what really works and what doesn't because the suggested medicines can sometimes be far more dangerous than the diseases they purport to cure. In an effort to sell their products, some advisers have proposed methods for achieving privacy that are either largely unworkable or downright perilous.

Dual Citizenship

Consideration should be given to the acquisition of more than one passport. In some cases, passports can legitimately be issued in different names. This opens the door to all kinds of possibilities — traveling anonymously, opening bank accounts in alternative names, and more. The acquisition of multiple passports of course presupposes that you are willing to accept multiple citizenship — and this is not at all a bad idea for many people.

With terrorism on the rise, international travel can be particularly hazardous to citizens of certain countries, the United States surely among them. Hostage-takers and kidnappers who have commandeered planes and boats have often looked at passports in deciding who shall live and who shall die. A second passport may also give you access to travel in countries where an American passport cannot be used because of U.S. State Department regulations.

For others, the benefits of a second passport may not be quite as pressing, but dual citizenship does nonetheless convey several advantages. Many nations have laws which restrict the purchase of real estate properties. Typically, coastal properties and those in large desirable metropolitan areas are off-limits to foreigners. Such practices have been widespread throughout Europe, Asia, South America — even in Mexico. Paradoxically, some of the available properties have remained unsold for long periods of time, not because they are outrageously priced but rather because locals could not afford to purchase them. The acquisition of a second nationality could be your key to living like a king or queen in one of the world's most desirable cities.

A major tax loophole allows Americans living abroad to exclude from taxes $70,000 of their earned income, and dual nationality may make it easier to establish a residence abroad. Other financial advantages of dual citizenship include the ability to purchase otherwise restricted shares in emerging foreign companies. Many foreign stocks and mutual funds are only available to local citizens. Issuers will require affidavits from potential buyers. Present the appropriate second passport as proof of citizenship and you are home free.

Employment is yet another issue. The United States has done little to discourage foreigners from jumping American borders and working in agricultural, manufacturing, and retail sectors. The number of undocumented aliens employed in the United States is staggering. In addition, Europeans, Canadians, and others who have special skills often obtain *green cards* from Immigration and Naturalization in order to legally establish residency and work in the United States. Tens of thousands of physicians, nurses, executives, technical specialists, and others do it every year.

Americans, on the other hand, are largely banned from working anywhere outside U.S. borders. Citizenship in another country can change all of that quickly. In fact many of the world's largest multinational corporations favor employment candidates with dual passports. If you set out to open your own business overseas, the same advantages will apply.

Finally, dual nationality could open all kinds of doors overseas including participation in foreign social security programs, national health programs, even university tuition remission programs. The specific benefits naturally depend on the country you choose.

The countries most often cited for dual citizenship include Great Britain, Ireland, France, Germany, Italy, the Netherlands, Austria, Canada, Mexico, and Jamaica. Others are Argentina, Brazil, Venezuela, the Bahamas, Bolivia, and Panama.

In most instances, governments only extend citizenship to individuals who have resided within their boundaries for minimum periods ranging from three to five years. These provisions can of course be waived. Few nations are begging for immigrants and those which encourage immigration are selectively looking for individuals who can provide specific services — like physicians, agricultural experts, entrepreneurs likely to create new jobs, and science teachers. After all, what possible benefit can a nation derive from wantonly issuing passports to outsiders with no purpose other than to skirt another nation's laws or to protect the privacy of individuals it hardly knows?

It is possible that you already qualify for a new passport by virtue of your ethnic background. If you are of Germany, Italian, Irish, French, or Jewish ancestry, it is likely that you are eligible. Other countries, however, are eager to naturalize those who do not automatically qualify especially if they can bring professional talent or expertise to their nations. If you have a distinguished career in teaching, engineering, general management, administration, or medicine, you have a decided advantage.

Several international firms claim to have connections which enable them to expedite the passport issuance process, obtaining dual nationalities for their clients in as little as two weeks. Sometimes this can be effected by bribing government bureaucrats, a common and accepted practice in many developing countries. You may be charged $5000 or more for these services with money passing through Swiss banks. Drivers licenses and other documents useful for identification can be obtained in the same fashion. In some cases, completely new identities can be established.

You should be a little wary of such claims. There have been numerous reports of swindles, however, hundreds of clients losing thousands of dollars each year on documents that are never issued. Stories also abound suggesting that some passport acquisition services have simply issued bogus credentials to their clients. If you find yourself in possession of forged travel documents, you could of course end up in prison for many years. Moreover, if the sole purpose of obtaining such documentation is to conceal your identity so that you can commit fraud or some other crime, or to hide a prior criminal record or divorce, you have merely compounded your troubles.

If you choose to pursue dual nationality through legitimate channels, you can probably obtain a valid second passport in a reasonably short time. Be sure to consider any adverse consequences, however. If your are a *naturalized* American citizen, you risk losing your American citizenship by swearing allegiance to another flag, voting in a foreign election, or deliberately renouncing your American citizenship at a U.S. embassy abroad. Native-born Americans will find that their U.S. citizenship is virtually cemented in stone

You might also be conscripted into the armed services of another nation if you happen to find yourself at the wrong place at the wrong time. Fortunately, many nations have moved towards voluntary armies — and if you're as unhealthy as the typical American couch potato, you need not worry anyway.

Renouncing Your Citizenship

Drastic a measure as it might seem, thousands of Americans and others renounce their citizenship in their native or adopted countries each year. The actual numbers are disputed, but it is widely known that the practice is becoming more widespread. People who chose this tactic are not criminals and they are not necessarily unpatriotic to their homeland. Often they are simply fed up with either the political or economic climate back home or more typically the money-grabbing practices of their government tax authorities.

Many Americans have become financially successful by accumulating enormous portfolios offshore. By investing in annuities and building equity in foreign corporations, they have been able to hoard large nest eggs free from taxation during many years of growth. Unfortunately, these savings only represent deferrals because the time eventually comes when they will want to enjoy the spoils of their sound investment policies and hard work. Distributions then become taxable back home. Others find it easier to get around this problem because their governments don't tax their earnings when their reside offshore. The United States government by contrast has long sought to drain every last penny from its citizens whether they reside at home or abroad.

Rather than share tens or even hundreds of thousands of dollars in taxes with a government which had nothing to do with their personal wealth accumulation, an increasingly large number of Americans eventually move offshore in their retirement years, renouncing their American citizenship and taking up residence elsewhere. Long-time permanent residents of the United States who are not American citizens have one less step to take to enjoy their wealth. They have merely to move overseas; renunciation of citizenship is not required (although recent tax law changes are making even this more difficult).

U.S. law does provide for taxation on U.S. source income for ten years after the renunciation of citizenship. The proceeds of foreign annuities, however, do not qualify as U.S. income and are safe from taxation. Thus an American living overseas can decide to renounce citizenship at any time, knowing that the ten year rule will have little effect on them. When citizenship is abandoned before death, the entire estate can pass free of inheritance taxes.

Establishing An Offshore Residence

For those people bold enough to undertake this strategy, dozens of domiciles exist worldwide. Consideration should be given to Panama, Costa Rica, Honduras, Guatemala, and Uruguay — all attractive and inexpensive places to live — if you prefer to stay in the Americas. None of these countries tax income from foreign sources.

The same kind of financial arrangements can be made for those who establish residency in the United Kingdom and Ireland. Once residency is established, however, further interest or dividend earnings *remitted to the country of residence* from offshore investments will become taxable. No taxes will be paid on capital brought into these states, essentially forgiving all taxes on gains made prior to establishing residency in the U.K. or Ireland. And the offshore nestegg can continue to grow with untaxed earnings that are not remitted to the respective country of residence.

Immigrants to Israel are granted exemptions on foreign-source income for the first seven years. Malta and Cyprus have also adopted laws severely reducing the tax burden on monies brought into their countries when used for normal living expenses. Monaco is another choice worthy of consideration, a small but vibrant nation with no income taxes.

For those who are able to invest heavily in real estate or pay rather hefty rentals, Campione may be both a tax haven and a personal heaven. Surrounded by and economically linked to Switzerland, Campione is really a little piece of Italy. Foreigners can easily obtain residence rights here, something not so easily done in Switzerland, and with open borders can travel freely to both Switzerland and Liechtenstein. Campione imposes no personal income tax or municipal tax. Its revenues all arise out of the operation of a local casino.

Becoming Your Own Banker

It has often been said that if you can't beat them you should join them. Offshore banking offers many rewards as already discussed here. Many individuals have taken the process one step further, opening their own offshore banks in an effort to achieve major tax and privacy advantages.

In many smaller countries, a bank can be chartered quickly and at relatively low cost, perhaps $25,000 or less. Compliance with local regulations as well as international treaties is still serious business, however. Governments are ever vigilant about outsiders opening banks in their jurisdictions which may well end up defrauding their own citizens. It is therefore essential to have adequate local legal representation before undertaking such a complex task. Forget about those do-it-yourself kits offered by quick-talking experts on international banking.

Americans pay hundreds of thousands of dollars each year for books and seminars promoting the benefits of opening their own banks offshore. The attraction is simple. Income from offshore banking is not currently subject to Subpart F taxation. When American citizens control offshore corporations, foreign income generally passes through to them much as it would in a traditional partnership. Banking income, however, is not covered by Subpart F so the earnings continue to accumulate at the offshore bank, free of U.S. taxes. Naturally, it is important to set up the bank in a country which has both low taxes and a favorable tax treaty with your home country.

One caveat which is not often mentioned by hungry own-your-own-bank promoters is that the IRS will disallow these advantages if the bank is deemed a sham, having been organized only to avoid taxes. In other words, the offshore bank must show that it conducts business in the real world, soliciting deposits from investors and making loans to others. The customers must of course be unrelated parties. In the absence of such a showing, the IRS will treat the bank as an offshore investment corporation, subjecting American shareholders to Subpart F taxation.

The United States is constantly pressuring foreign banking authorities to tighten their laws and bank charter requirements, making it more difficult for Americans and others to set up new banks in their nations. Besides the start-up costs involved in organizing the bank, expect to invest at least $250,000 and perhaps as much as $1,000,000 or more in working capital, depending on the location selected. Even if the bank conducts most of its operations by mail, it will need some sort of office or store front location, minimal staff, equipment, and supplies. The use of captive offshore banks for lawful tax avoidance purposes makes sense only for the wealthiest investors.

Mail Drops And Remail Services

Far less radical methods for concealing your whereabouts are available worldwide. One of them is the use of a mail drop or mail forwarding service. Instead of using your own home or business address for correspondence, you in effect rent an address with a business that specializes in accepting mail for absentee clients. These services offer far more than the mere convenience of mail acceptance. They provide a simple means of maintaining your privacy.

The United States Postal Service offers post office boxes at virtually all its post offices. Unfortunately, the agency requires that you furnish proof of your actual street address before issuing a box; furthermore, under the Freedom of Information Act it will furnish that address to anyone who asks for it, defeating the whole purpose of keeping your address confidential.

Commercial mail drops and mail receiving and forwarding services by contrast usually ask no questions. For a small monthly fee, they will provide you with a street address which looks like a physical location. It may contain a suite or apartment number for sorting purposes, far less suspicious than a post office box number. You can pick up your mail in person or the service can routinely forward it anywhere you request. You pay the additional postage in the latter case.

If you travel frequently, you don't want your mail to accumulate at your home or business or worse at the post office. For reasons of personal safety, you may also not want others to know your true physical address. Another powerful reason for establishing a mail drop is to protect against government snoops. It is common practice both in the United States and abroad for government authorities to request *mail covers*. Simply put, postal carriers are instructed to record the return address of all mail they deliver to your address, filing the information with law enforcement or tax authorities. Agencies may be especially interested in mail you receive from international correspondents including banks, brokers, and other financial institutions.

Even more onerous is the increasing surveillance of the contents of envelopes mailed through the postal system. This ostensibly requires a court order in the United States but the practice is also widespread in other countries where police have greater independence. Sophisticated techniques allow envelopes to be opened and resealed with no apparent evidence of tampering. The application of solvents can render ordinary envelopes translucent, allowing intruders to read the contents; when it dries, the envelope again becomes opaque. In other words, you may never know that you have been spied upon. In some instances, envelopes may simply be slit open and then delivered to you as if they had been inadvertently misdelivered to another address first.

One huge exception to the requirement for a court order in the U.S. is that foreign mail may be opened without a warrant. It is not legally considered first class mail, and the search is legally equivalent to a customs search at the border. Even the reading of contents is authorized under this legal theory, and there are people serving prison sentences based on cases in which evidence was gathered in this way. Yet the average American is firmly convinced that their mail cannot legally be opened by government agents.

Although you can take ordinary precautions like asking your correspondents to omit return addresses, use security envelopes printed with black patterns inside, or double-envelope and tape all important mail, you are still at considerable risk. By using a commercial mail drop known only to your important personal and business associates, you can protect your incoming correspondence from unwanted intrusions. If you travel extensively, you may want to establish mail drops in locations that you frequent.

Interestingly enough, the concept of mail forwarding for purposes of maintaining anonymity has now extended to the Internet. Numerous *anonymous remailers* have been established by benevolent organizations committed to the principles of privacy. Normally, when email is sent over the internet, the recipient receives the message together with a lengthy *header* that clearly identifies the sender and the path the mail has taken in its travels. By using an anonymous remailer, usually available at no charge to either the sender or recipient, the electronic mail is devoid of any information which can be traced back to the true sender.

Speak Softly

Lastly, you should not overlook the obvious. Many breaches of privacy result directly from personal carelessness. The Internal Revenue Service has been known, for example, to monitor the activities of American citizens to determine whether their lifestyles and spending habits appear compatible with their reported incomes. In recent years, turncoat agents showed up at both FBI and CIA headquarters; they would probably never have been discovered except for the fact that they started driving Mercedes Benz sedans and buying expensive real estate clearly beyond their reported means.

The less your neighbors and colleagues know about you, the better off you are. A few careless comments at the bank or barber shop can cost you dearly. There are some important guidelines to follow. Never disclose more information than you have to give up. If you are applying for a credit card with a nominal credit line, there is no reason to divulge all the sources of income you might have; provide only enough information to achieve your objectives. If you apply for a mortgage on real estate and you have sufficient equity in the purchase, it may be to your advantage to pay a slightly higher rate in exchange for a loan that requires the submission of no income or net worth information. Keep in mind that any information you furnish can and probably will be shared by the lender with others.

If you are thinking about marriage, consider the efficacy of a prenuptial agreement. It will not only protect your assets in case the marriage needs to be dissolved in the future, but it may also help insure that personal financial information remains private in the event that a divorce occurs.

In the event you are happily married, make certain that your spouse and children don't inadvertently share confidential information with others. A frank discussion at the dining room table is in order to make sure everyone understands his or her responsibilities and obligations..

Finally, if you employ others in your business, make certain that you require them to enter into legally *enforceable* non-disclosure agreements so that your financial and trade secrets remain secret during and after their period of employment. Such agreements should include serious sanctions for any potential breaches.

Chapter Twelve

Technology: The Death of Privacy

When O. J. Simpson took to California freeways in what has come to be known now as a *low-speed chase,* a really strange oxymoron, local police were on his tail thanks in part to his use of a cellular phone. Ever since that fateful afternoon, local and national law enforcement agencies have been clamoring for more. They now want to require cellular telephone companies to install more sophisticated triangulation equipment so that the location of cellular-equipped vehicles can be pinpointed with extreme accuracy. With cellular phones nearly standard equipment for many drivers, Big Brother will soon be able to track your every move.

It is all reminiscent of one of the stupidest criminals in history, a man who recently dialed 9-1-1 to advise his local police department that he had planted a bomb in a nearby building. Having called from his own home, his address was immediately displayed on the 9-1-1 dispatcher's monitor and twenty minutes later he was arrested.

Telephone Privacy

Many local phone companies throughout the United States now offer their subscribers *Caller ID* service or an enhanced *Caller ID with Name* service for a small additional monthly charge. The idea is that a local subscriber can check his display to see who is calling before he answers the phone. If he is away and misses the call altogether, he can check his display to see who called, even if no messages were left on his answering machine.

Authorities soon discovered that social workers and investigators who often used their personal phones to call others in the community had lost their privacy. Phone companies were ordered to block Caller ID technology for these people. Thousands of others came forth, demanding the same anonymity. The chess game began in earnest. Today you have the option of pressing a few digits before making a phone call to prevent others from knowing who is calling. This service is usually referred to as *Caller ID Blocking*. The phone rings but the display shows nothing. Perhaps later subscribers will be able to order *Caller ID Blocking Defeater* to prevent callers from blocking identification.

Whether or not you use Caller ID, however, the digital nature of today's phone services in most American communities allows the phone company, and consequently law enforcement agencies, the luxury of tracking your local as well as long-distance calls. In many exchanges, you can punch up a few digits to record the origin of the last call you received, useful when obscene or threatening callers invade your privacy. The number is normally not disclosed to you, only to police upon your request. Although this service may seem at first glance to offer protection against harassment, the technology can easily be turned around to keep tabs on your incoming as well as outgoing phone calls. At one time, only long distance toll calls left any paper trail. With today's digital telephone technologies in place, *any* call may leave a paper trail. If you use your phone for critical personal or business reasons, you are at grave risk of losing your privacy.

Do not become too complacent thinking that you have an unlisted telephone number. It is probable that the number has already circulated to hundreds if not thousands of telemarketers. This is largely an American problem because obtrusive telemarketing has not yet become an international dilemma. The invasion of one's privacy by telephone would be considered unthinkable in many other parts of the world where a man's home is still his castle.

America Online (AOL), the nation's largest broad-based online service with more than 8 million subscribers, announced in July 1997 that it was going to provide its members with what it termed a new *benefit*. It was going to sell its members' phone numbers to its *advertising partners*. According to AOL president Steve Case, the new program would allow members to buy all kinds of products and services at discounted prices.

In plain language, 8 million members would be in jeopardy of receiving telephone solicitations at their homes or businesses.

The move came as little surprise to many observers because AOL, in its quest to expand its customer base, had already engaged in very questionable practices. In December 1996, it introduced an unlimited use program for its members at a flat rate price. Its computers and telephone access lines became so overburdened that millions of its members were unable to connect at all. The attorneys general of more than 30 states joined together on behalf of their constituents and AOL was forced to make a financial settlement. A few days after the proposed telephone marketing program was disclosed, AOL buckled under pressure and rescinded its decision. Nobody wanted the *benefit* of privacy invasions.

The problem is that AOL, like credit card companies and other American institutions, usually require the disclosure of telephone numbers at the time accounts are established. They then recklessly sell or lease these numbers to other advertisers, a strong source of revenue. Subscribers to online services are particularly vulnerable because these providers might also furnish other information to list brokers such as the Internet sites regularly accessed by its customers. This might give third parties clues as to your lifestyle, business and personal interests, and finances.

Americans who travel or live outside the borders of the United States can protect themselves against such unwanted intrusions by using offshore Internet service providers rather than American-based companies that have extended their tentacles worldwide. European companies are far less likely to engage in such dubious practices. In addition, they cannot be forced to disclose to American authorities any information arising from Internet use or email activities. The FBI is constantly serving court orders on U.S.-based Internet service providers to probe the activities of their subscribers.

The smaller problem of simply avoiding telephone solicitations can be handled inexpensively in several ways. One of the easiest is to install more than one telephone line in your home, keeping each one unlisted. There's a good chance you have already done this to accommodate your computer or fax machine. Whenever a service vendor like a credit card company requests a telephone number, give them the one used exclusively for non-voice transmissions — and make it a practice *never* to pick up this phone to answer a call. After repeatedly receiving a fax carrier tone or no answer at all, callers will get the message.

Several states have prepared *no-call lists* to which you can subscribe for a nominal fee. Vendors are expected to cross-check their prospect lists with the no-call lists before beginning any telemarketing program. Telephone solicitation to people who have asked not to be called them becomes a criminal offense. Unfortunately, special interest groups have again made their way to state legislatures, gaining exceptions for themselves. Newspapers circulation departments, real estate agents, and charities have been granted exemptions from the *no-call list* rule in Florida, a state that otherwise levies heavy fines for telephone solicitation violators.

Personal Intrusions By Greedy Businesses

A few years ago, several American supermarket chains began subscribing to one of several tracking services to learn more about the buying habits of their customers. Patrons were offered the opportunity to earn rewards for shopping at their stores. All they had to do was sign up by filling out a rather lengthy profile which elicited demographic information about themselves and their families — ages, educational levels, annual income, housing statistics, and more. Whenever they shopped, they would simply present their bar-encoded discount cards to the store cashiers who scanned them before ringing up the merchandise.

Most folks never got back more than a few dollars or some discount coupons after many months of participation, but they gave up more privacy than they could ever have imagined. Corporate information collectors could now sell data bases replete with names, addresses, telephone numbers, the most personal family and financial information, even the brands of shampoo the subscribers purchased. If you thought that nobody knew you had a dandruff problem, you were dead wrong.

Every week in large city newspapers and Sunday supplements, other information collectors bait consumers with similar surveys. In return for answering a couple of hundred questions about your buying habits, your hobbies, your family income and demographics, you are promised an envelope full of useful store coupons. Of course your name goes on nationally distributed sucker lists.

The *New York Times* recently did a feature story about a Massillon, Ohio woman who returned home from work one day only to find a twelve-page hand-written letter in her mailbox. The letter, replete with all kinds of sexual fantasies, seemingly detailed every fact of the woman's private life — the magazines she read, the brand name of the soap she used, even a reference to her earlier divorce. It turned out that the letter writer was a convicted rapist and burglar serving time in a Texas state prison.

The State of Texas had signed a contract with Metromail Corporation, a seller of personal marketing information, under which inmates would enter information from consumer questionnaires into computer data bases. A rapist was now in possession of information on the Ohio woman and thousands of other people whose data he had processed.

When the woman brought suit against Metromail, citing what she believed was an unlawful invasion of privacy, company executives went back to their own data bases, carefully extracting 25 pages of information on the plaintiff — everything from her income to the brands of products she purchased. According to the published story, Metromail budgeted $1.5 million to fight the case which has now become a class action. With annual revenues approaching $300 million, the firm has a lot to lose if held accountable for its actions. Soon after the lawsuit was filed, lawyers for Metromail conducted a seven-hour deposition of the plaintiff in which they asked for her social security number, unlisted telephone number, dating and drinking habits, and health history, among other things.

A local judge threw out the case against the prison. Under current law, most states grant themselves what is essentially sovereign immunity. The case against Metromail continues to work its way through the courts. The plaintiff claims that she should have been informed that prisoners were going to be assigned to process the survey she had voluntarily completed. She seeks compensation for her distress and injunctive relief to prevent such practices from continuing. Texas law provides for judgments arising out of "extreme and outrageous" conduct that causes severe emotional distress. Attorneys for Metromail argued that the Ohio woman's mere receipt of lascivious mail from a convicted rapist did not rise to this standard. Only time will tell who owns such personal information and what safeguards information repositories are expected to provide.

Although Metromail says it no longer uses prison labor, inmates across the country continue to have access to personal and confidential files of all kinds. Texas still allows prisoners to have access to sensitive records including motor vehicle information, state hospital patient progress reports, divorce decrees, even criminal investigation reports. Inmates routinely input data into computer systems or microfilm images as part of their assigned prison jobs. Public information is treated every bit as carelessly as privately-collected information.

Several states have contracted with hotel chains and car rental companies, establishing telephone reservation centers behind steel bars. Next time you give your credit card number to a mild-mannered telephone clerk in order to guarantee a reservation, consider that you may be talking to a convicted embezzler or burglar supposedly doing *hard time*.

Suffice it to say, too, that this could only happen in the United States. Felons serving time in prisons around the world do not routinely have access to the personal and financial records of those outside prison bars.

They're more likely to be slamming sledge hammers, making small stones from big rocks.

Inmates aren't the only ones collecting or disseminating private information. Although their motives may be somewhat different, police departments also play a role in collecting information that ought to remain private. Local law enforcement agencies in cooperation with merchants frequently conduct sessions in shopping malls where children can be photographed and fingerprinted. The program, purportedly designed to help authorities identify children who are later kidnapped or abducted, wouldn't be so bad if parents remained the sole owners of the completed fingerprint cards and portraits. Unfortunately, the vast majority of child abductions are undertaken by parents themselves, usually in response to unfavorable custody rulings. In some jurisdictions police are now suggesting that these fingerprint cards remain on file with them for safekeeping.

Adults may also be unwittingly tricked into giving fingerprints. In order to reduce their losses from bad checks, several large retail chains now require that personal checks be accompanied by a thumb print given with a new inkless technology. Several banks are requiring the same kind of identification when cashing checks for people who are not their regular customers. They point out that it is a simple, clean, and painless process. Of course it is also a gross and dangerous invasion of privacy.

The Federal Bureau of Investigation already maintains fingerprints on hundreds of millions Americans and others. Most of them are not criminals, but in the course of doing everyday business more and more fingerprint cards are being accumulated. In many states, fingerprinting and photographing are required for the issuance of professional licenses — everything from medical to real estate licenses. It is not as if the fingerprints are merely used to ascertain that the applicants do not have criminal records which would prevent them from being licensed. The fingerprints are then catalogued alongside those of convicted criminals.

The same is of course true of anyone who has been arrested in the United States. The fact that a jury has cleared a defendant of all wrongdoing does not in any way remove his fingerprints or photographs from local and federal repositories. In a few isolated cases, however, courts have compelled local and federal authorities to physically destroy such documents when it had been shown that government agents exercised gross misconduct in making arrests resulting in the original fingerprinting and photographing of defendants. Such a record-burning exercise in Oklahoma City a few years ago was ordered to the chagrin of law enforcement authorities.

Spying And Mind Control

High-tech equipment is now available through several large mail order firms to eavesdrop on others. One highly-directional microphone is said to pick up whispers more than 500 feet away. Video cameras disguised as books or radios can be purchased and placed throughout your home, allowing you to monitor your child's babysitter. Shop at any Wal-Mart and the large smoky plastic globes mounted throughout the store remind you, if the sign on the front door didn't, that you are under constant video surveillance. When you add those annoying bogus announcements every fifteen minutes that say something like "Security, monitor and record area 36," you realize that someone is constantly looking over your shoulder.

Cameras now routinely record the movement of people in American retail stores, banks, airports, parking garages, post offices, bus stations, and government buildings. You will also find video and audio recording equipment in some of the most unlikely places. Signs posted throughout a major performing arts center in Tulsa for years boasted that conversations were being monitored by hidden devices.

Police in many states monitor the roads from aircraft, ostensibly to check for speeders and other traffic violators. The technology now exists to monitor your every movement from satellites with photographic resolution so fine that images can be examined for facial features.

Technology has not only provided methods for more intrusive surveillance. It has yielded methods for controlling our behavior. Several years ago, researchers experimented with subliminal advertising in movie houses. Twin side-by-side theaters ran the same film with one slight modification. For the experimental group of movie-goers, single frames were spliced into the film, each one showing concession items such as cold beverages and buttered popcorn. A single frame lasts about one sixteenth of a second. The control group in the second theater received no such messages.

Even though single frames of film could not be seen, or more precisely consciously perceived, concession sales in the experimental theater far exceeded the control group. For a few short years it seemed that advertisers were going to jump on the bandwagon and proceed to introduce such subliminal messages in theaters and perhaps on television.

The law eventually intervened, putting a stop to such practices before they really got off the ground. More than thirty years have passed since that era and several large American retail chains have begun experimenting anew with what they say are harmless subliminal messages. This time they are audio messages, buried deep beneath the music in their stores. For the most part, they urge consumers not to shoplift. Researchers claim that they have been able to effect moderate reductions in pilferage. Who knows, in a few years retailers may start using subliminal messages to get you to buy athletic shoes or sugar-free desserts.

Computer Privacy And Encryption Technologies

If you use a computer in your personal or business life, the threat to privacy is even greater. Many software manufacturers make it easy for you to register the purchase of their products on-line using a toll-free telephone number. It saves time and postage. What you may not know is that some unscrupulous vendors use this opportunity to examine your computer's hard drive to determine what other software you have already installed. It's a process worthy of CIA operatives and a flagrant abuse of your right to privacy.

In 1997, flaws were discovered in one of the most popular web browsers published by Microsoft Corporation and used by millions of Americans and others overseas. In short, the reported defects allow web site operators to invade the computers of all those who access these sites. The operators could then freely search your disks for sensitive data, copying whatever they want. If you use software for preparing your individual or corporate tax returns, your most private information can be quickly compromised. Others could even insert viruses to cripple your machine if they are really intent on doing damage.

Send e-mail to a friend or associate just down the street and there is a good chance that it will be intercepted by a hacker at one of the dozens of sites through which your message typically passes in cyberspace. The Internet is an elaborate network of service providers with little protection against invasion. Send e-mail across the oceans and there is an even stronger possibility that your message will be screened by government computers for key words. Intelligence agencies have purportedly begun routine examinations of all trans-Atlantic communications. In an effort to drive CIA and NSA agents crazy, thousands of academics and others committed to preserving privacy rights routinely insert words like *Ghadafi*, *Iran*, *Iraq*, *bomb*, *cocaine*, *IRA*, and *explosives* in extraneous paragraphs within their email.

The point of all of this is very simple. We need ask ourselves what price we are willing to pay for a society free of crime, drugs, or money laundering. Many people are willing to allow their governments to expand wiretap capabilities. What if it was taken one step further? What if you learned that every telephone in your home had become an open microphone which allowed authorities to spy on you at will, even when the phones were hanging on their cradles?

In the cat-and-mouse game between government and individuals bent on privacy, an entire new industry has sprung up. It is the industry of *encryption software*. Once available only to governments and corporate giants determined to keep their trade secrets secret, it is now possible for anyone to send absolutely secure email across the world, literally unbreakable by the world's most sophisticated intelligence agencies. The same technologies can be used to scramble you computer's files, making them totally unusable should your computer ever be stolen, sent in for service, or in the worst case scenario, seized by authorities. Just keep in mind that if you ever have a stroke and forget your password, your secret files are locked forever. The only way the government would be able to crack your files would be to put you on a medieval rack and stretch you until you provided the code or *key* as it is technically called.

The most foolproof system for computer or communications encryption is based on PGP technology. Developed by Phil Zimmermann, PGP (short for Pretty Good Privacy) is a system which utilizes a highly sophisticated technology in which two *keys* are used to decrypt a message or computer file. When used for e-mail, the sender needs only one key to encrypt the message. The recipient then decrypts the message with a second key which is itself installed on his computer and password-protected. Such encryption systems can be used to send letters, digitized photographs or illustrations, bank records, music, voice communications, or anything else which can be sent electronically across telephone or internet channels.

A number of commercial encryption programs are also available. Not nearly as secure as PGP, but sometimes more user-friendly and well worth the investment, are a couple of titles you should consider: Norton's *Your Eyes Only* or an Elementrix product called *Power One Time Pad (POTP)*. These can be used for encrypting e-mail over the Internet as well as individual files or entire directories in your computer. Another excellent program is *Stealth Encryptor*, published by Tropical Software, currently available for less than $30.00. It offers several encryption options including DES technology for both files and email. *Stealth* utilities, incidentally, are used to hide files on a computer, scrambling not only their contents but their file names. This software also provides a shredder utility to completely obliterate Windows files; when merely deleted in the usual manner, Windows files are still usually recoverable from a hard disk even after you think they have been erased.

If your personal computer were ever stolen, sent to a shop for repair, or even seized by government agents, its contents could fall into the hands of unscrupulous people. If you maintain personal, private, or financial records on your computer — or send such records to others by electronic mail — encryption is almost a necessity.

You should keep in mind that the American government has already made efforts to limit access to programs like PGP. This should not surprise you because files encrypted with software of this strength are unbreakable by even the most sophisticated computers available to the intelligence community. It is already a federal crime to export PGP outside U.S. borders. Authorities tried unsuccessfully to prosecute Zimmermann when they learned that PGP had found its way onto the Internet and was being distributed worldwide.

Today the program is available at no cost, downloadable from many Internet sites and is in very wide use throughout the world. PGP's export from the United States has been banned for several years but its import into the United States poses no problem. The software has already found such wide application overseas that it is rumored the U.S. government may soon be compelled to license its export.

If you have access to the Internet, you can use search engines like Yahoo or Alta Vista to locate current sites for downloading the program. Alternately, you can obtain PGP from many commercial sources which have constructed interfaces specifically for DOS, Windows, Windows 95, and Macintosh platforms. It may be advisable to acquire PGP or another encryption program as soon as possible because governments may try to take further steps to limit their availability.

The Clipper Chip

Big government, intent on limiting privacy, has proposed an alternative means to allow individuals and businesses to encrypt messages sent over telephone lines. Although the technique may prevent other individuals, businesses, or competitors from spying on you, it leaves the encryption keys in the hands of government proxies. The National Security Agency (NSA) and the National Institute for Standards and Technology (NIST) jointly designed something called the *Clipper Chip*. Like all sophisticated encryption techniques including the now-popular RSA, DES, and PGP protocols, the Clipper Chip would allow users to assign encryption keys which are long series of numbers. Armed with the proper keys, message recipients would then rely on the chip's internal algorithm to decode the encrypted messages and make them readable.

The Clipper Chip was designed with a secret encryption algorithm known as Skipjack. Master keys capable of decoding any messages encrypted under this system would then be placed in escrow The algorithm would be stored on two separate decoder keys, each 40 bits in size, and each stored with a different government agency. In theory, local or federal law enforcement agencies would have to request the two keys in order to decode electronic messages, presumably going to court to show probable cause that a crime has been committed.

More frightening is the fact that telephone companies would be required to feed telephone communications to some sort of central monitoring station where the government would maintain decoding capabilities for those transmissions encrypted with the Clipper Chip. Digital files which were encoded with alternative programs, those for which the government maintained no keys, would of course stick out like proverbial sore thumbs. If the government were to pass legislation outlawing alternative encryption methods, the net effect would be the irreparable destruction of individual privacy once and for all. Big government would have keys to every home and every business.

Proponents of the Clipper Chip argue that safeguards would protect innocent individuals and businesses, that the technology would only hamper the effects of drug dealers, international terrorists, and other criminals. We know, however, that Uncle Sam and some of his counterparts overseas cannot be trusted to maintain any safeguards that might accompany new legislation enabling agencies to expand their spy capabilities. Before we know it, Clipper Chip keys would find their way into the hands of law enforcement agencies on mere fishing expeditions.

Unlawful government spying has been a bipartisan practice for many years. The Nixon White House vigorously spied on its enemies in an effort to secure reelection. It went so far as to authorize and then cover up the now-infamous Watergate Hotel break-in. The Clinton White House abused its power when hundreds of supposedly protected FBI files were released to political operatives. We cannot forget former FBI Director J. Edgar Hoover who interpreted his job description to include his agency's mandate for spying on prominent Americans including members of Congress and religious leaders like Martin Luther King. Domestic spying has been a bipartisan activity for decades.

Although many Americans have been duped into believing that high-tech inventions like the Clipper Chip will ultimately provide for a safer society, most constituents recognize such a slippery slope when they see one. It is unlikely that enabling legislation will be forthcoming any time soon, educated Americans fearful of having the fox guard the henhouse. The Clipper Chip would be tantamount to handing over the keys to your home and business to well-meaning government agencies which promise to keep them safe and secure.

Chapter Thirteen

Tomorrow May Be Too Late

Doomsday prophets aside, many astute economic and political analysts have begun drawing bleak pictures of what the future holds. Although many of us might prefer not to believe them, there may be a world of truth in what they are telling us. Nobody knows with certainty what tomorrow will bring, but careful and thoughtful analyses of recent trends suggest that the worst may be yet to come.

Banking networks which are now teetering on disaster may crumble under the weight of regulatory systems that severely impede their ability to function. Government rules and reporting requirements drain hundreds of millions of dollars out of the system every year. The U.S. dollar is in immediate danger of faltering under a bankrupt economic system plagued with national debt and frightening trade imbalances. The individual's ability to exchange currencies freely on world markets or to place dollars in foreign banks could be banned altogether. Social engineers will continue to design and implement more far-reaching tax programs to take money from those who have it in order to give it to those who don't.

Some people say that a police state is just around the corner as civil liberties continue to erode. Assets seizures, already all too common, will continue to grow at an exponential rate. Local and national law enforcement agencies have already discovered that seizures represent one of the easiest means to fill their coffers. Why should they stop when due process is so easy to set aside, monies flowing in freely? Virtually anyone who finds himself falling out of the good graces of Big Brother can become a target.

The Abuse Of Taxpayers

In 1988 a Taxpayer Bill of Rights was adopted by Congress and forced on the Internal Revenue Service in response to complaints about IRS agent abuses. When Congress attempted to strengthen its provisions in 1992 in response to continued complaints, bills got bogged down in both houses for months. Unfortunately, the law turned out to be little more than a useless credo. The legislation required the IRS to do a number of little symbolic things. First, it was told to prepare a simple statement of taxpayer rights. Today it hands out a silly little brochure to all taxpayers who find themselves in conflict with the agency.

The bill created a new position at the IRS, the Assistant Commissioner for Taxpayer Services, as if the 115,000 person bureaucracy wasn't already top-heavy enough. It imposed new penalties which were totally out of tune with reality. As an example, the unauthorized disclosure of taxpayer information by *preparers* could result in civil penalties of $250 for each infraction. It provided for a number of specific instances where taxpayers could request the Tax Court to reopen cases to resolve discrepancies. On a macro basis, it did nothing to restraint IRS from its most notorious practices.

Every few years, Congressional critics of the IRS muster enough courage to challenge the agency's procedures publicly. It takes courage alright because the IRS has been known to retaliate harshly against its critics. Presidential candidate Steve Forbes even suggested the abolition of the Internal Revenue Service during his 1996 campaign. Only time will tell whether his magazine empire falls under scrutiny of a repressive IRS audit.

In any case, several Congressional watchdogs caused the General Accounting Office (GAO), the government's internal auditor, to conduct a detailed investigation of Internal Revenue Service practices. In October 1994, the GAO reported its findings to Representative Steny H. Hoyer,

Chairman of the House Subcommittee on Treasury, Postal Service and General Government. They were shocking to say the least.

The agency which it said was "responsible for administering our nation's voluntary tax system" had indeed committed a wide array of taxpayer abuses that went well beyond the expected abuses institutionalized by law. "We found an example," the GAO wrote, "in which an IRS employee, after accepting a cash payment from a taxpayer, stole the cash payment and falsified the document used to credit the taxpayer's account."

It also said the it "found various instances of what we consider to be taxpayer abuse by IRS. Some instances involved situations in which IRS employees violated either the law or IRS Rules of Conduct and the taxpayer abuse may have been intentional." That seemed like pretty harsh comments coming from an internal auditor. Imagine what an independent outside audit might have revealed.

Furthermore, the GAO wrote that it "also found that the controls to prevent IRS employees from embezzling taxpayers' cash payments relied to a great extent on employee integrity and taxpayer complaints." It described in detail taxpayers whose bank accounts were levied after IRS employee misappropriated payments or otherwise committed gross fraud.

Referring to one specific case, the GAO said that "Internal Security investigated her complaint and determined that the IRS collection employee whom she paid had embezzled most of her cash payment by altering the amount on the cash receipt he submitted to the collection support staff. This employee also embezzled other taxpayers' cash payments for which he had not submitted any cash receipts."

Much of the picture painted by the General Accounting Office was of an agency whose left hand didn't know what the right hand was doing. In several cases the agency set out to collect from various businesses, some of them already bankrupt, withholding taxes that had either never been collected or remitted to the IRS. Under the law, the IRS can impose severe penalties as high as 100 percent of the unpaid taxes, not to mention interest. These penalties can be levied against business employees and officers deemed to have been responsible for the shortfalls.

Scores of individuals complained to Congress that they had been wrongfully targeted by the IRS for these penalties. In some cases, low-level bookkeepers who had nothing to do with collections or remittances were harassed for months. In the end, *they* had to show cause why they shouldn't be penalized. In other cases, the IRS concurrently went after a multiplicity of employees in its aggressive efforts to collect taxes it believed were due, each employee unaware of all the others who had been victimized.

The GAO also took issue with the manner in which the IRS conducted audits. "When selecting taxpayer returns for examination, IRS often uses computer-generated lists to identify returns with examination potential. However, because computer-aided selection techniques rely solely on information in filed returns, IRS collects information from outside sources to identify other areas of potential taxpayer noncompliance. Information Gathering Projects (IGP) are one technique that IRS uses to collect outside information and to identify returns with examination potential."

At first glance, it seemed that the auditors were talking about IRS 1099 forms and the like, but as they proceeded with their report they finally became more explicit. "If someone contacts IRS with information that a taxpayer has not reported a substantial amount of his or her income and suggests that an audit could be warranted, that information would be referred to the Examination Division in the IRS field office that has jurisdiction."

In layman's terms, the GAO was referring to the Snitch Division. If you have a neighbor or colleague in need of punishment, write the IRS.

As scathing as the GAO report was, it accomplished nothing. For starters, the Internal Revenue Service simply disagreed with many of its findings.

The General Accounting Office had shared a preliminary draft of its report with the IRS's Acting Commissioner prior to its final release.

In its final report, the GAO said that "IRS disagreed with our recommendation that it establish a definition of taxpayer abuse and identify and gather the information needed to systematically track the nature and extent of such incidents. IRS said use of the term *taxpayer abuse* was misleading, inaccurate, and inflammatory; disagreed with parts of the definition of abuse used in our study; challenged the assumption that there was any additional need to collect additional information about abuse and asserted that the problem, to the extent it exists, was well under control."

Of course taxpayers continue to be hauled into IRS offices for fishing expeditions. Individuals and businesses charged with tax violations are still presumed guilty until they prove themselves innocent. The American tax system simply affords no respect to taxpayers. It is in no uncertain terms unlike any other tax collecting authority in the world.

Plan Early To Get A Head Start

It is never too early to start planning for the new order. Many American families, relying on the advice of medical and psychological specialists, now encourage the optimal developmental growth of their young children by taking early aggressive steps. We put mobiles in their cribs, read to them at bedtime long before they can comprehend language, and start them in day care or preschool programs at the earliest possible time. Some folks even advocate that expectant mothers should be surrounded with appropriate music to promote stronger fetal development.

We teach our kids the importance of early learning and thrift. For more than two centuries, American parents have adopted a tradition, setting aside resources for their children's education and future. Some begin to fund college costs when their children are born. Several states have enacted annuity programs for just this purpose. Piggy banks and real bank accounts are today considered an integral part of growing up. Many young children already own stocks, bonds, and mutual funds.

As we get older we hopefully start providing for our own futures, investing wisely through diverse vehicles. Virtually every financial adviser suggests diversification as they key to a bright future. Many of us check our Social Security Administration records every couple of years, verifying that contributions have been properly reported, at the same time requesting an estimate of benefits payable at retirement age. (Corrections for uncredited contributions can only be made for three years.)

Unfortunately, all of this effort could be for naught. A number of trends in monetary, fiscal, political and social policy emerging in Washington and elsewhere, if taken to their natural conclusion, leaves us with a gloomy and frightening portrait of tomorrow. It is no longer safe to rely on old adages and techniques to guarantee a comfortable future.

The issuance of national identity cards may become a reality for Americans in the very near future. They will arise under the guise of national security or the need to bolster immigration law compliance. One day it may be impossible to cash a check, take a book out of the library, or buy an airline ticket without such a card. With one unique number assigned to every adult and child in the United States, it will be easy for government agents to track every aspect of your life. They will know how much you spend, where you travel, what you read. Your personal and financial records will be wide open for government inspection at any time

Government Is Unpredictable

It's been said that the only two things we can be sure of are death and taxes. Although many western nations including the United States have had relatively stable governments, i.e., the absence of full-scale revolutions, life today is anything but predictable. This applies equally well to Congressional legislation, administrative policy making, and judicial review.

Special interest groups play a far bigger role in shaping our society than rank-and-file citizens.

Dr. Jack Kevorkian, America's champion of the right to die with dignity, knows far better than anyone else what it is like to live in a community where government bureaucrats decide to target someone for prosecution or more aptly, persecution. While polls show that the vast majority of Michigan voters have steadfastly rejected the idea that governments have the right to order us to suffer unbearable pain and agony, local prosecutors continued to go after Kevorkian, tooth and nail, to win a conviction for assisted suicide.

When they realized that a temporary Michigan law specifically written and enacted to target Kevorkian had expired and that he could not be found guilty of any *statutory* violation, prosecutors charged the retired pathologist with *common law* criminal violations, a practice unheard of in the United States. His attorney, Jeffrey Feiger, argued to the jury that the state had essentially made up a law in its vindictive attempt to put Kevorkian away. The jury agreed and found him not guilty. If you were charged under some purported unwritten common law, would you be so lucky so as to escape conviction?

Later in 1997, the U.S. Supreme Court held in a landmark decision that the U.S. Constitution does not specifically convey the right to assisted suicide. It threw back to the states the right to regulate the matter. The question now remains whether special interest groups will get to their state legislatures before the people speak their minds. If this trend continues, terminally ill patients in great pain will soon have to travel across state lines or even national borders to end their suffering.

Lower trial courts have been every bit as unpredictable as the U.S. Supreme Court in meting out justice in both civil and criminal matters. Just outside Plantation, Florida, three teenagers were charged with manslaughter following their alleged removal of a traffic sign from a local roadway. A vehicle carrying three other teens sped through the intersection where a stop sign once stood. Their car was hit by a truck, killing all of its occupants. The tragic accident happened about two weeks after the sign was felled. The sign was still laying on the ground at the time of the collision.

The defendants admitted having gone on an earlier spree, removing other signs as trophies. Each however vehemently denied having tampered with the stop sign whose removal from the ground caused the accident. Not even the state alleged any intent by the defendants to cause harm but the prosecution nonetheless sought sentences of 25 to 50 years imprisonment.

The state's circumstantial case hinged on the expert testimony of several paid expert witnesses who said the stop sign *must* have been uprooted by hand since it showed no signs of having been hit by a vehicle. A prosecuting attorney made it a point to walk up to the jury box to show gruesome autopsy photographs in order to prejudice the jury.

Although there was not one shred of physical evidence linking the removal of the stop sign to any of the three defendants — no fingerprints, no witnesses, no hard evidence — a jury quickly convicted them of manslaughter. Following their conviction, sobbing members of the victims' families pled for harsh punishments, spewing religious rhetoric. Families of the defendants pled for mercy, bringing their own clergy. They also pointing out the young ages of the three convicted felons. This kind of public spectacle in which sentences are influenced by emotional pleas instead of rational justice is becoming ever more popular in American courts. The judge ultimately sentenced each of the three to fifteen year terms in the state penitentiary with fifteen additional years probation. Shock waves quickly spread through the legal community.

A few weeks after the verdicts were rendered and punishments proclaimed, several local resident came forth to say they were sure that a large service vehicle that had been operating at the intersection had in fact knocked the stop sign out of the ground. One of the state's witnesses also recanted his testimony, stating that a prosecutor had threatened him in order to coerce favorable testimony against the three defendants.

It's no wonder that many local as well as federal prosecutors claim one hundred percent conviction rates. District attorneys, particularly those who are elected by blood-thirsty constituents, are more interested in high conviction rates than any search for the truth. The American judicial system is very flawed.

The same week the three alleged vandals were convicted, the state continued to release scores of convicted felons, murderers and rapists among them, a move mandated by prison overcrowding. Some had served just a small fraction of the time for which they can been committed. And while murders and rapists were hitting the streets, the state was also busy committing hundreds of others convicted for victimless crimes including prostitution and possession of marijuana. American legislators have a fix for all of this, of course. Taxpayers can always fund more prison construction in a nation that already has the world's highest incarceration rate, more than one million Americans currently locked up in jails or prisons.

The unpredictability of governments, particularly in court actions, underscores the problems that individuals and businesses face every day. In a highly-publicized case, a man who lost his job with Miller Brewery successfully sued his former employer and a coworker whom he said was responsible for his firing. Although he was employed under an arrangement that in theory allowed his employer to terminate him at will without cause, he alleged that he had been unfairly fired and sought damages. His firing had followed an accusation of sexual harassment by a female colleague. The man had joked about an episode of the popular sitcom *Seinfeld* which had aired the night before on network television, the show's theme replete with humorous sexual overtones.

Not only was he awarded more than twenty-five million dollars in damages against his former employer, but he also won a $1.5 million judgment against the woman who had reported her claim of sexual harassment to her management in the first place. Nobody except the parties involved in the dispute really knows what happened or whether the man's conduct rose to the level of sexual harassment. We have learned, however, that civil awards in the United States often show no relationship to actual damages sustained by plaintiffs. This is especially true when defendants maintain a high profile like O. J. Simpson or have deep pockets typical of the largest corporate litigants.

In California, state legislators looked to Washington for inspiration in adopting what has come to be known as "three strikes and you're out" legislation. A defendant who has already been convicted of two felonies, even if they occurred ten or twenty years earlier, now faces life imprisonment for a third conviction of any magnitude. The third crime could be shoplifting a pack of cigarettes or smoking an illegal joint, but mandatory sentencing now dictates a life sentence for a third offense. An armed bank robber who shoots and paralyzes a teller during the commission of a bank holdup will probably receive a far lighter sentence than a *third-strike* defendant who grabs and steals a six-pack of beer from a convenience store.

With respect to privacy rights, American law has been turned on its head with few exceptions. Alleged victims of sexual assault and rape are protected by so-called rape *shield laws* which allow them to remain anonymous from newspapers, the tabloid press, and mass media reporters. These well-meaning but unbalanced laws were enacted to protect true victims from being victimized a second time by the system and all of its attendant publicity.

But what happens to a defendant who is ultimately acquitted of such charges? During his ordeal, he receives no public protection against false accusations, his name and photograph typically splattered all over the front pages of newspapers. Even if he is acquitted of all wrongdoing, the person who made the allegations is entitled to remain anonymous. Front-page defamation may eventually be followed by two-inch articles buried deep in local newspapers pronouncing these acquittals. Legal scholars justify this practice, reminding us that defendants who are found not guilty of a crime have not been proven innocent. The state has merely failed to meet its burden of proof beyond a reasonable doubt.

Let us not forget Richard Jewell who was vilified by the FBI in its rush to judgment to find someone responsible for the Atlanta bombing during the Olympics. Federal agents went so far as to try to trick him into giving up his constitutional rights against self-incrimination, fabricating a story that they wanted him to participate in making a training video on bomb investigations. Such a training video was of course never contemplated. Authorities were willing to use any ruse necessary to make a case.

In testimony before a Congressional oversight committee, a representative of the Justice Department's Office of Professional Responsibility said that *strategic deceptions* were often used by FBI agents to extract information. Instead of hailing Jewell as a hero for saving lives in Centennial Park, the FBI under the direction of the U.S. Attorney General's office ruined an innocent man's life. And when the suspect, finally cleared of any wrongdoing, began suing the media that had libeled him, exacting several quick out-of-court settlements, commentators quickly labelled him a *professional plaintiff*.

The presumption of innocence before trial (and for those acquitted of crimes, after trial) is a myth. It's no wonder so many wealthy people succumb to private extortion attempts rather than let their cases proceed to trial. The government can and does play havoc with the lives of people it doesn't like. What most Americans learn about their judicial system in high school civics classes bears little resemblance to what happens in the real world. Despite what you may have been taught to believe, justice is likely to be more even-handed in dozens of countries outside the United States.

If you plan to start up a business, you should carefully consider the implications of competing legal systems, particularly if you intend to employ others. The benefits of doing business offshore should not be overlooked. You will not face the ever-increasing burdens of federal, state, and local reporting requirements in most jurisdictions abroad. Tax issues aside, American businesses must routinely file reports on occupational safety and health issues as well as a host of Equal Employment Opportunity (EEO) compliance matters relating to hires and terminations. Many of these reports then become public record, opening the door to lawsuits by money-hungry litigants.

When you do business in the United States, you may be sued if you fail to create or maintain a balanced work force with an adequate representation of minorities. This applies not only to racial and ethnic composition but to gender. People over forty years of age may sue you under federal age discrimination laws. So can the handicapped. You could be forced to spend tens or even hundreds of thousands of dollars to alter physical facilities to accommodate employees and customers with a myriad of handicaps and special needs. It is tantamount to disaster running an American business without the counsel of seasoned labor and civil rights attorneys.

You can never be sure what a court might rule in a particular civil action. In the last three years, the table has been turned in various discrimination suits. People who had been denied employment or admission to universities because those institutions admitted less qualified minorities have now successfully prosecuted suits for discrimination. With the President and Congress fighting over affirmative action, and voters in states like California passing referendums on the issue, American business owners are left suspended in air, vulnerable whatever courses of action they take. American unpredictability is a precursor of the decision by many entrepreneurs to take their businesses offshore.

Freedom — The Endangered Species

Many of George Orwell's predictions did not come to pass by 1984, but he was surely right about the role Big Brother would play. Individual freedoms and privacy have been badly abridged already, and they continue to erode with each passing day.

On retrospect, America's founding fathers might have actually had a good inkling of how miserable government could make our lives. Although they could never imagine the explosion in technology, the Bill of Rights seemingly covered every possible contingency to protect us against government tyranny. Unfortunately, they had no way of knowing that the first ten amendments to the Constitution would eventually be twisted and shaped into something grotesquely different from its intended objectives.

The framers of the Constitution of the United States and later the Bill of Rights clearly understood the consequences of arbitrary searches and seizures. They must be turning in their graves today, knowing that the explicit due process protections they afforded all Americans are all but gone now. Seizures, searches, and forfeitures are as common today as the British taxes on American trade which led to the Boston Tea Party.

The presumption of innocence was once believed to be a major asset of American jurisprudence. Prosecutors were expected to prove us guilty beyond a reasonable doubt before the state could take our life, liberty, or property. Today property confiscations by federal, state, and local agents are rampant — and in virtually every case, the accused is required to prove his innocence in order to get a shot at reclaiming his cash, securities, real estate, or other forfeited valuables. The deck has been so stacked against the individual that it is rarely possible to prevail in such situations using traditional legal tactics.

What is perhaps most troubling is the fact that many Americans have become so accustomed to the rhetoric coming out of Washington that they willingly concede their Constitutional rights in the name of *law and order* or a *drug-free society* or some other abstract principle. The exercise of one's Constitutional rights is *not* a "loophole" of justice. It is what once kept all of us free of governmental tyranny.

Public outrage followed the murder of young Jon Benet Ramsey in Boulder, Colorado. Much of that outrage was immediately misdirected by press reports that the parents had refused to be interrogated by police detectives. Consider, however, the heavy-handed tactics of the police who had literally threatened to hold the victim's body hostage, refusing to release it for burial until the parents acquiesced to their demands. When that threat failed, local police and prosecutors started trying the case in the media, leaking all kinds of innuendo in an effort to get an upper hand. Unlike almost anywhere else in the world, American trials are often conducted before juries of public opinion instead of impartial juries of one's peers. Such judicial misconduct could never happen in most of the rest of the developed world.

Also consider that the United States Supreme Court has ruled that police may blatantly lie to suspects, even telling them that there are witnesses or evidence which does not in fact exist, in an effort to extract confessions. The *good cop, bad cop* game is as popular today as it was at the turn of the century. What lawyer in his right mind would permit a suspect or defendant to waive his Fifth Amendment right against self-incrimination and talk freely to authorities? A defendant, whether guilty or innocent of a crime, has absolutely nothing to gain by consenting to an interrogation.

Public outrage should be directed instead at incompetent law enforcement authorities which clearly bungle criminal investigations every day, not the people who exercise precious constitutional rights granted to *all* Americans. As soon as we begin picking and choosing who is and who is not entitled to invoke constitutional guarantees such as the right to remain silent, we throw ourselves into a cesspool of danger.

Courts have upheld the right of employers to conduct pre-employment drug tests. At one time, this authority was restricted to specific classes of workers like airplane pilots and train engineers where a clear showing of possible public harm could be made. American courts soon extended the practice wantonly, allowing all employers to conduct pre-employment tests as well as random testing during the terms of one's employment.

Individuals who have been prescribed legitimate drugs for conditions ranging from tendinitis to impotence must either disclose their use of such medications or risk being denied employment or being fired. Of course, the of disclosure of a medical condition itself predisposes the individual to losing his job. Most Americans who work for others these days do so under a doctrine which presupposes that the employer may terminate them at will for any cause or no cause at all.

Perhaps local police or even landlords will be authorized by the courts next year to conduct random drug tests in our homes and apartments. Our precious liberties, the ones we once thought set us apart from the rest of the world, the ones our father fought so hard to achieve more than 200 years ago, are slowly but surely being carved away one at a time.

Promises, Promises

Finally, consider the fact that you have no reason to trust government to carry out its promises. If you are in your forties, fifties, or sixties, you have been paying into the Social Security trust fund for years — just over $10,000 in 1997 if you were self-employed and earned $65,400 or more. This figure does not include an additional 1.45% of gross earnings paid to the Medicare fund, not subject to any ceiling.

You probably considered Social Security to be an insurance program, believing that the proceeds of your lifelong investment in the plan would be available at retirement. Instead, at a time when many people are thinking of retiring earlier than ever before, the normal early retirement age has been pushed back. Depending on your year of birth, you may not be eligible for full retirement benefits until you are 66 or 67 years old. Congress has looked at pushing it back still further. The same is being considered for Medicare eligibility.

Imagine what your reaction might be if such unilateral changes were imposed on the annuities or life insurance policies you bought from private insurers. *Breach of contract* means nothing to government. You can't sue Washington for breach of contract and you shouldn't be surprised if the rules of the game keep changing. Governments grant themselves *sovereign immunity* — a term which simply means that they are exempt from complying with rules of conduct expected of everyone else. They do as they please.

Add to all this bad news the fact that earnings tests have already been imposed on Social Security old-age fund recipients. The more you earn, the less you receive from Uncle Sam. The government is intent on kicking older people out of the work force to make room for younger people. This makes sense because all the good commercial and industrial jobs are going overseas, largely in response to oppressive American taxes.

The worst is yet to come. Many observers believe that an asset test will soon be applied in determining whether retirees receive Social Security benefits at all. If you have been smart enough to earn and invest your money wisely, you may one day be barred from collecting benefits under the Social Security system on the grounds that you are too rich. It won't matter that you contributed to the fund your entire working life.

Individual states are now getting into the act of sharing your private pension benefits, too. If you receive monthly distributions from an employer-sponsored retirement plan, the state where you lived at the time you were employed may be looking to you for the payment of income taxes — even though you haven't lived in its jurisdiction for years. Court challenges to this new practice have so far been unsuccessful.

Politicians keep talking about tax reform. The idea of a flat tax has been debated widely. So has the application of value added taxes in place of income taxes. No matter how you slice it, some governments are forever growing and consuming more and more revenue. It is just a question of *how* they will take your money. Your right to move money across national borders, regulated as it already is now, could become far more restrictive. All sorts of exchange controls could be imposed on short notice, severely curtailing your ability to protect your assets by investing offshore. Your government could order the repatriation of overseas funds, forcing dollars out of foreign banks and stock holdings.

Drop Your Pants, You're About To Board An Aircraft

Millions of Americans have for years undertaken all kinds of efforts to remain transparent in the eyes of their government. Fed up with continued intrusions by Big Brother, many have gone underground, not filing taxes in years. Others have developed more law-compliant methods of remaining transparent, like the methods discussed in this book. But now the Federal Aviation Administration has proposed a method of its own to actually help you in your bid to become transparent.

In a letter to Vice President Albert Gore dated February 11, 1997, eighteen prominent Americans representing major civil liberties, privacy advocacy, legal, and religious institutions vigorously protested new proposed FAA rules for the traveling public. The letter was written under the auspices of the Electronic Privacy Information Center, a public watchdog agency that seeks to protect citizens from all privacy abuses in both the public and private sectors.

Among the proposals was one which called for the installation of special high-tech X-Ray cameras in American airports. Developed with FAA funding, these special scanners literally take pictures of those who pass their lenses as if they were completely undressed, revealing the most intimate details of their anatomy. It's the latest craze proposed by Washington, the electronic strip search. Naturally, White House lawyers will find some way to deflect criticism that such equipment violates the Fourth Amendment right against unreasonable searches. The same government lawyers have undoubtedly argued that *Playboy* and *Penthouse* publications should be removed from airport newsstands because their photos are too revealing.

Security issues aside, your right to travel freely may not remain sacrosanct. The list of countries off-limits to travel by Americans can be expanded quickly by Congressional action or administrative decree. Americans are banned from travelling to Cuba and Libya today; perhaps Switzerland and Grand Cayman will be on the list tomorrow. Bureaucrats will decide who may travel and for what reasons.

With respect to domestic travel, the FAA issued orders in 1985 effectively demanding that airlines require all passengers to present government-issued photo identification documents before boarding planes. The ostensible reason was airport and in-flight security. It has been reported that a number of families travelling with small children were denied boarding because the children did not carry photo ID cards. One might ask whether a potential bomber would be so stupid as to show a true driver's license or passport in any case.

An unrelated proposal now before Washington bureaucrats was purportedly developed to help airlines and government investigators notify families of victims of air crashes. It would require, among other things, that airlines obtain the true name, date of birth, and social security number of each passenger on a domestic flight, recording this information on a passenger flight manifest. Imagine the long-term consequences of such a program. The government would effectively create another massive database, enabling it to track its citizens as they travelled from one city to another. It's the next nearest thing to fitting all Americans with electronic tracking bracelets or requiring all automobiles to carry identification transponders. We might also expect the government to impose the same requirements on railways and bus operators in the not too distant future.

By contrast, Europeans still enjoy relatively unencumbered travel. People who pass in and out of European airports often see soldiers armed with machine guns, a rather disconcerting sight for Americans. Passengers are also expected to take reasonable precautions such as staying with their luggage at all times to prevent tampering by potential terrorists. On the other hand, travellers pass freely from country to country within the

European Union. They are not subjected to extensive immigrations and customs searches as in the United States and they certainly do not give up their privacy rights the moment they arrive at an airport.

Then there is the matter of proposed expansions to the government's *profiling* programs for airline passengers, both domestic and international. Not only would names, dates of birth, and social security numbers be mandated but the information would be combined with data bases showing home addresses, locations of previous flights, the manner in which airline tickets were purchased and paid for, and previous criminal records. It appears that arrest rather than conviction records would be used, a gross violation of one of the most basic tenets of American justice — that an arrest means absolutely nothing until and unless a conviction has been achieved. This proposal is particularly troubling in view of the fact that FBI records, by the agency's own admission, are inaccurate a whopping 33 percent of the time.

Conceivably, people who purchased their tickets with cash would become particularly suspect. So would those with certain names, perhaps those of Middle East origin. Persons who frequented selected destinations that fell out of favor with Washington would become prime targets for denied boarding or worse, criminal investigation.

Many wealthy business people and other well known public figures have for years chosen to fly incognito, going so far as to use personal disguises and tickets purchased under assumed names. People known to have assets and those with high public profiles legitimately have reason to fear criminal acts including robbery, extortion, kidnaping, and murder. Well known men and women from the worlds of business, banking, entertainment, sports, and religion often have to contend with menacing crowds. Some have been forced to fly with bodyguards.

Still others have to fight off the press wherever they travel. Experience of course teaches us that government data bases are anything but well protected. Even the National Crime Information Center (NCIC) database is routinely misused. Ask any tabloid editor and he will tell you that he has *sources* who can access NCIC whenever needed. By requiring travelers to use their true identities, the government is literally putting their lives in jeopardy whenever they travel on scheduled airline flights.

Justice William O. Douglas wrote in Kent v Dulles (1958) that "the right to travel is a part of the *liberty* of which the citizen cannot be deprived without due process of law under the Fifth Amendment." That was forty years ago. We can't be too sure what travel rights may remain tomorrow.

Privacy Implications For Families

Whether you take conservative or more aggressive efforts to protect your own privacy, you should also think about related family issues and the potential benefits that offshore residency may provide. The American government has intruded into virtually every aspect of life for American families. Foreign travellers to the United States are often amazed at what they see. Take the case of a young European-bred mother who recently visited New York with her young child. While dining with the child's father at a local restaurant, she left the toddler in its carriage just outside the restaurant's window in a protected area and in clear view from her table, a common practice throughout Europe.

Police were called to the scene. Lacking any kind of sensitivity or cross-cultural finesse, they immediately arrested and jailed the parents overnight, and placed the youngster in protective foster care. Both the parents and child were needlessly traumatized. In part, this is of course a commentary on the American crime scene, but moreover it depicts the ugly and intrusive nature of today's government. The U.S. State Department ultimately got involved in the dispute when the woman's own government protested vigorously. Charges against the woman were eventually dropped, conditioned upon her deportation from the United States.

In some cities, American parents who spank, scold, or otherwise discipline their children are subject to prosecution for child abuse. American families are torn apart every day by overzealous social workers bent on dictating how we are to raise our children. In all fairness, it should be pointed out that similar intrusions are becoming popular in a few other places, notably Scandinavia, where welfare states flourish, and governments dictate how parents are to raise their children.

Few foreign governments, however, have usurped parental rights in the way it has been occurring in the United States. The parents of a child who shows up at school with bloodshot eyes following a breakfast reprimand for unacceptable behavior is likely to end up these days at the principal's office or at the local police station. Schools are legally bound to report suspected cases of child abuse or neglect and are protected from liability even when they make reckless reports to authorities.

Newspaper accounts of modern-day witch-hunts in which entire communities of adults have been charged with the sexual abuse of their children have surfaced recently. Self-styled therapists, under the direction of law enforcement agencies, methodically created memories in children of events that ultimately were proven to have never occurred. Anyone who runs a day care center today needs to have his head examined.

More benign but nonetheless worrisome breaches of family privacy are much more common. A business acquaintance tells the story of his child's first day in public school in Ohio. The teacher asked her pupils to stand up, one at a time, and say a few words about themselves. She went so far as to ask several of her students to disclose what their parents did for a living. One girl said her father was a fire fighter. Another five-year-old said that her mother was a librarian. Then came the statement from my friend's young boy. His parents, for many years having been concerned with personal privacy, had already prepped their child for such a contingency. He stood up and proudly told his class that both his parents were *reliable sources*. Bringing up and educating your children offshore once seemed like an extreme measure. Today, it makes more sense than ever.

School isn't the only place where your children can get you into trouble. A number of parents have been hauled into court when local photo finishers observed perfectly innocent family snapshots of nude children frolicking in or around their homes. The film processors, the latest addition to the community of public snitches, immediately alerted authorities. When the parents showed up to retrieve their prints, they were arrested, handcuffed, and taken before local magistrates. Among other things, American parents now have to fear the police when they let their children swim nude in their private backyard pools or run through the privacy of their own homes undressed.

In another case, photographic processors observed what they thought were pieces of stolen art in the prints they had prepared for a wealthy local resident. They reported the matter to authorities who quickly raided the apartment. It turned out that the framed paintings were nothing more than reproductions legally acquired by their owner. The search warrant was ruled to have been issued on the basis of probable cause, the homeowner having no recourse against the police. There may be some very pervasive reasons for having your film processed overseas. At a minimum, consider using electronic digital photography, Polaroid technology, or video reproduction — none of which require outside processors.

Laws requiring various institutions to snitch on their patrons are not all targeted at children. Several states now require hospitals to report *suspected* cases of domestic violence — and *suspected* is the operative word. Patients who show up in emergency rooms with injuries that hospital staff believes may have been caused by other family members, despite assurances by these patients to the contrary, must now notify local authorities. The government, in its effort to protect us against ourselves and our families, has created a chaotic mechanism in which thousands of Americans are required to defend themselves each day against unwarranted accusations.

One of the most objectionable practices of government is the comprehensive census conducted by the U.S. government every ten years.

One of its purported purposes is apportionment, allowing Congress to design voting districts which give the people fair and equal representation in the House of Representatives. We all know that apportionment has become a process in which Congress gerrymanders districts into absurd geographic slices in order the maximize the majority party's chances of gaining seats in the next election.

For the individual, the census creates a far more serious problem. Americans are compelled to answer each census under the threat of a contempt citation. If you are unfortunate enough to be randomly selected to receive a *long form*, you may be required to provide information ranging from personal income to the number of flush toilets in your home.

We are told, on the one hand, that justice is color blind yet we are required by law to disclose *race* among other things on the census. A controversy currently rages as thousands of people of mixed heritage refuse to be pigeonholed into one of the specific race categories provided on census questionnaires. One pundit recently suggested that one of the choices for race be *human*.

Theoretically, the U.S. census can only be used for statistical purposes. Information on individual households can never be disclosed to anyone under government regulations. In addition, the Code of Fair Information Practices and the Privacy Act provide that information furnished to the government for one purpose is not to be used for another without the specific consent of the individuals to whom the information pertains. These provisions are so routinely violated by government agencies as to make the commitment of privacy meaningless. Besides, the actual gathering of census data is conducted by tens of thousands of part-time census workers who receive little more than a few days of training. Any suggestion that U.S. census operations ensure privacy is little more than a myth. Nowhere in the world does any other census operation parallel the intrusive nature of the census you face every ten years.

Plan Today, Not Tomorrow

Whatever your current financial situation, it is not too early to begin contingency planning for the unexpected. You should consider the worst case scenario as well as the most probable scenario in deciding on appropriate strategies to protect your assets and your way of life. Among other things, you should make portfolio diversification a high priority, making prudent offshore investments to preserve your assets in the event of a personal or national economic catastrophe. It is not enough to diversify by buying a multiplicity of U.S. stocks or bonds. If the dollar ever fails, you could be economically destroyed.

The probability of being named as a defendant in a civil action increases with each passing day. The more you own, the greater your vulnerability. A judgment sufficient to wipe out a lifetime of asset accumulation could result from an unintentional automobile accident, a serious injury sustained by a guest on your property, a mispoken word, or a bad business decision. It might well occur as a result of nothing you have done. The judicial system is often totally arbitrary and capricious. Will your personal and business assets be sufficiently protected against such creditors?

Equally important, you should explore all avenues which protect your privacy, making it difficult if not impossible for governments or private creditors to seize your hard-earned assets. And although history shows that individuals exert little influence over their governments, if you are an optimist you should take a more active political role in the hope that you can shape your own future and that of your children.

Realistically, things will get worse and not better. Even if you move many of your assets offshore in order to protect your privacy and your wealth, you should keep a careful eye on political and economic changes abroad. Washington will persist in bullying smaller nations into submission. Some will surrender, forcing you to again transfer assets across borders, but others will continue to exercise resolve, determined to keep privacy and other personal freedoms alive.

Going offshore, either financially or physically, may be your best move if you relish privacy and care about preserving your accumulated wealth.

About the Author

Adam Starchild is the author of over twenty books, and hundreds of magazine articles, primarily on business and finance. His articles have a appeared in a wide range of publications around the world — including *Business Credit, Euromoney, Finance, The Financial Planner, International Living, Offshore Financial Review, Reason, Tax Planning International, Trusts & Estates*, and many more.

His personal website on the Internet is at http://www.cyberhaven.com/starchild

www.ingramcontent.com/pod-product-compliance
Lightning Source LLC
Chambersburg PA
CBHW021938220326
41599CB00010BA/522